COLUMBIA UNIVERSITY STUDIES IN
ENGLISH AND COMPARATIVE
LITERATURE

DRAMA AND LITURGY

DRAMA AND LITURGY

BY

OSCAR CARGILL

1969
OCTAGON BOOKS
New York

Reprinted 1969
by special arrangement with Columbia University Press

OCTAGON BOOKS
A DIVISION OF FARRAR, STRAUS & GIROUX, INC.
19 Union Square West
New York, N. Y. 10003

AM

LIBRARY OF CONGRESS CATALOG CARD NUMBER: 73-86272

Printed in U.S.A. by
TAYLOR PUBLISHING COMPANY
DALLAS, TEXAS

TO MY

FATHER AND MOTHER

PREFACE

Professor Thorndike once remarked, when we were discussing this study, that "the trouble with the liturgical theory is that it is too *pretty*." The very adequacy of the theory had earlier aroused my suspicion: it is rarely that we find an explanation for anything in life or art so complete and perfect, as the one advanced by Magnin and Sepet for the medieval drama. I began in a small way, and partly out of curiosity, with the *Secunda Pastorum*, endeavoring to show that little masterpiece to be wholly the work of a wide-awake artist and not the result of growth. From this play my interest naturally broadened and this study is the result.

One of the pleasures of this sort of labor is the acknowledgment of friendly and critical aid. To Professor W. D. Briggs, of Leland Stanford University, and Professor John S. P. Tatlock, I am indebted for encouragement in my earliest researches in the drama, whilst I still held orthodox views. Professors Hoxie N. Fairchild, of Barnard College, and Carey H. Conley, of Wesleyan University, have examined certain MSS for me. The Reverend Acton Griscom has also furnished me with valuable suggestions in regard to several manuscripts. I am especially indebted to the librarians of Cambridge University, the British Museum, the Bibliothèque Nationale, the New York Public Library, the Library of Cornell University, the Library of New York University, and the Library of

Columbia University, for the privileges granted, and the kind aid given me.

Mr. Matthew Peacock, of Oxford, England, has supplied me with facts about Wakefield; Mr. R. A. Pilkington, of Eccleston Grange, Lancashire, has endeavored to find Gilbert Pilkington for me. Professor G. P. Krapp, of Columbia University, has shed light on several difficult philological problems. Professors F. A. Patterson and H. M. Ayres, of Columbia, have read and offered suggestions on my manuscript. My colleague, Professor Margaret Schlauch, of New York University, criticized to my advantage one of the earlier drafts of this study. Professor Louis Wann, of the University of Southern California, permitted me to examine his notes on the Towneley MS and brought to my attention the fact that the Towneley Library was founded by Sir Charles Towneley. Professor Ashley H. Thorndike was the first to recognize the possible merit of this projected study, and has, throughout its course, been a profitable and considerate friend and adviser. But to Professor W. W. Lawrence unquestionably I owe most. For five years he has given generously of his time and scholarship to the progress of this investigation.

O. C.

New York City,
November, 1929.

CONTENTS

ix

Chapter I

PRELIMINARY SURVEY

The Period of Speculation and the Discoveries of Magnin

The purpose of this study is to direct attention to the inadequacy of the so-called "liturgical theory" to account completely for the origin of the mystery plays. The wide and enthusiastic acceptance of this theory, as well as its apparent sufficiency, have long deterred scholars from a minute examination of its merit. In fact there appears to exist not even a mild challenge of its truth. Now it should be conceded even by the most ardent supporters of any theory that the subjection of their case to criticism is of considerable positive value. At all events, this query is begun in a humble search for truth, rather than in any spirit of contentiousness.

Though the liturgical theory is so well known that people less scholarly than Macaulay's schoolboy have it by heart, it is imperative that we should refresh our minds with its essential features here:

During the ninth and tenth centuries the germs of modern drama appeared in the elaborate ritual of the Easter service in the greater cathedrals and monasteries of Europe. The dramatic liturgies thus evolved consisted originally of a few lines of question and answer chanted responsively by priests, and taken almost literally from the Vulgate Latin lesson for the day. The following lines of dialogue from a ninth century manuscript of the Swiss monastery of St. Gall comprise the simplest version extant of the so-called Easter "trope":—

> "Quem quaeritis in sepulchro, Christicolae?"
> "Iesum Nazarenum crucifixum, o caelicolae."
> "Non est hic, surrexit sicut praedixerat.
> Ite, nuntiate quia surrexit de sepulchro."

A century later the *Concordia Regularis* of St. Ethelwold (ca. 980) furnishes the first document dealing with the drama on English soil, in a set of directions for the acting of a Winchester trope differing only in the slightest details from that of St. Gall.

In imitation of these Easter celebrations, bits of choral dialogue, likewise beginning with the words "quem quaeritis," were early devised for insertion into the services of Christmas and Ascension Day. Once introduced, the dramatic element in the liturgy became widely popular and rapidly extended itself. Harking back from the Christmas play of the Saviour's birth, characters and events from the Old Testament were introduced by way of prologue or forecast, while at the same time the Easter and Ascension plays developed sequels dealing with the reign of Antichrist and the Final Judgment. It was but a matter of a century or so till the two sets of plays, presenting respectively the birth of Christ, and his resurrection and ascension, had grown to meet each other and fused into a complete religious drama embracing the history of the Bible from the Creation to the Judgment Day.[1]

Though work on the details has been done by many eminent scholars, the actual formulating of this theory is due to the labors of two men, one working nearly a century ago, the other addressing himself to our grandfathers. Charles Magnin, lecturing at the Faculté des Lettres de Paris, in 1834, first declared that the Latin liturgy was the source of the mysteries; and Marius Sepet, in 1867, in the most important book published up to that time on the

[1] C. F. Tucker Brooke, *The Tudor Drama,* Boston, Houghton Mifflin, 1911, p. 2.

drama, *Les Prophètes du Christ*, advanced a novel and fascinating hypothesis which made it possible to believe that every scene of the plays was a growth from, or a duplication of, material already existing in the liturgy of the church. Despite the fact that neither Magnin nor Sepet was a medieval scholar, their conclusions have apparently remained unchallenged since the time they wrote. Many a student might be envious of their good fortune.

Prior to the suggestions of Magnin, all sorts of notions were rife as to the origins of the medieval drama. The critics were to some extent in accord in postulating a lay source for the plays, although they varied widely as to the precise character of that source and as to the details of development. Moreover, these earlier theories of origin, although due to scholars who merely touched upon the drama in more general works, were at least formulated by men better versed in the Middle Ages than either Magnin or Sepet. While the French poet, Boileau (1636–1711), did not enjoy this distinction, he was perpetuating a popular tradition of great antiquity:

> Chez nos dévots aïeux le théâtre abhorré
> Fut long-temps dans France un plaisir ignoré.
> De pèlerins, dit-on, une troupe grossière
> En public, à Paris, y monta la première;
> Et, sottement zélée en simplicité
> Joua les saints, la Vierge et Dieu par piété.
> *Art poétique, Ch. III, 81–86.*

The Abbé La Rue (1751–1835), author of a study of the troubadours, bards, and jongleurs, stated it as his positive opinion that the jongleurs first fashioned the mysteries in the early part of the twelfth century.[2]   Thomas Warton

---

[2] *Essais historiques sur les bardes, les jongleurs, et les trouvères,* Caen, Maniel, 1834, 3 vols, Vol. I, Art. II, p. 158 ff.

(1728–1790), who never documented his proof closely enough to satisfy modern critics, but who swept over an immense field in his researches, advanced the following theory in his *History of Poetry:* [3]

About the eighth century, trade was principally carried on by means of fairs, which lasted several days. Charlemagne established many great marts of this sort in France; as did William the Conqueror, and his Norman successors, in England. The merchants, who frequented these fairs in numerous caravans or companies, employed every art to draw the people together. They were therefore accompanied by jugglers, minstrels and buffoons; who were no less interested in giving their attendance, and exerting their skill, on these occasions. As but few large towns existed, no public spectacles or popular amusements were established; and as the sedentary pleasures of domestic life and private society were unknown, fair time was the season for diversion. In proportion as these shews were attended and encouraged, they began to be set off with new decorations and improvements; and the arts of buffoonery, being rendered still more attractive by extending their circle of exhibition, acquired importance in the eyes of the people. By degrees, the clergy, observing that the entertainments of dancing, music and mimicry, exhibited at these protracted annual celebrities, made the people less religious, by promoting idleness and a love of festivity, proscribed these sports, and excommunicated the performers. But finding no regard was paid to their censures, they changed their plan, and determined to take these recreations into their own hands. They turned actors; and instead of profane mummeries, presented stories taken from legends or the Bible.

The views of Boileau, La Rue, and Warton are representative of the state of critical opinion before Professor Charles Magnin announced his theory. Taking a hint perhaps from Frontenelle [4] (1657–1757), Magnin declared in the

---

[3] *Op. cit.*, Vol. III, pp. 193, 195.

[4] See La Rue, Vol. I, p. 168; also note 11 below.

course of his lectures, in 1834, that the tropes were really Latin plays, and that from these the mysteries developed.[5] The Roman Church, he believed, was the source of the medieval drama, just as the Greek religious rites were the source of the drama of antiquity. Imagine the immense interest in the Latin liturgy his conjectures created among scholars! Almost immediately there began the publication of numerous texts of an antiphonal nature from the liturgy

[5] "La savante et ingénieuse critique de M. Charles Magnin a fait nettement ressortir le lien, vaguement entrevu avant lui, qui rattache les mystères du moyen âge à la liturgie catholique." Marius Sepet, *Les Prophètes du Christ*, p. 1.

For Magnin's work on the drama, see the "Cours à la Faculté des Lettres de Paris," *Journal de l'Instruction publique*, for the year 1835–36; various articles in the *Journal des Savants* (1846) pp. 1–16; 76–93; 449–65; 544–58; 626–37; (1847) pp. 36–53; 151–62; (1860) pp. 309–19; 521–40; (1861) pp. 481–503. Also: *Histoire des origines du théâtre moderne, Paris, Prolégomènes*, 1838.

Inasmuch as I could nowhere obtain copies of the *Journal de l'Instruction publique* for the year 1835–36, I have not examined that periodical. There seems to be no doubt, however, that Magnin was the first to work out in detail the theory which identifies the tropes with the drama and assumes that the mystery plays evolved from the liturgy. Compare, for example, the following passages from *Les Origines*, pp. ii and xxiii:

"Oui, le génie dramatique a toujours existé en France; seulement son langage, son allure, ses interprètes, étaient bien différents de ce qu'ils sont aujourd'hui. Les prêtres chrétiens, désespérant d'extirper du coeur des grands et du peuple la passion des fêtes et des représentations scéniques, songèrent de bonne heure à s'emparer de l'instinct dramatique, à le diriger vers les choses saintes et à le faire servir à augmenter l'attrait des cérémonies de l'église. . . .

"Dès l'ouverture de la troisième période, nous verrons le drame ecclesiastique obligé de renoncer à la langue latine et de la remplacer par des idiomes vulgaires. Devenu peu à peu trop étendu pour conserver sa place dans les offices, le drame liturgique fut représenté les jours de fête, après le sermon, etc."

together with the texts of Old French plays.[6] No close, comparative scrutiny of these texts was made, however, to test Magnin's theory, because what he had asserted seemed so obvious. One realizes the tremendous influence of Magnin, not only by the fact that his utterances awakened a popular interest in these texts, but also from the appearance of Pierre Gringoire, reputed author of mysteries, as a literary character, in the first chapters of Victor Hugo's *Notre-Dame de Paris*.[7]

Now Charles Magnin was the perfectionist of savants— an eighteenth century idealist born too late.[8] Idealism breathes through his introductions, as it must have animated his lectures:

Do not listen to me as a pleader in favour of this date or that, more or less doubtful, [for the appearance of the drama]. I believe neither in the awakening nor the slumber of human faculties; I believe in their continuity, especially in their perfectibility and in their progress.[9]

[6] Prior to Sepet's work were published: Monmerqué et Michel, *Théâtre français au moyen âge*, Paris, Delloye, 1839; Achille Jubinal, *Fragment de la resurrection*, Paris, Techener, 1843; Edéléstand DuMéril, *Origines latines du théâtre moderne*, Paris, Franck, 1849; Luzarche, *Adam, drame anglo-norman*, etc. Tours, Bouserez, 1854; Coussemaker, *Drames liturgiques du moyen âge*, Rennes, H. Vatar, 1860.

[7] *Notre-Dame de Paris* appeared in 1831; but Magnin and Hugo were well acquainted. Francisque Michel says that Magnin had been "occupied a great number of years in profound study upon this subject." (Monmerqué et Michel, p. 1). I believe I am the first to point out the influence of Magnin on Hugo. I am not hardy enough to assume that the relations were reversed.

[8] Cf. John Morley, *Rousseau* (London, Macmillan, 1900), Vol. II, p. 119.

[9] *Les Origines du théatre moderne*, Paris, Hachette, 1838, Vol. I, p. ii.

We can readily see how a man holding pronounced views as to the perfectibility of the human faculties might, as a scholar, be prone to find illustration of these views in his studies. Such apparently existed in the transformation of the trope into the mystery play. Yet Magnin withal was a profound classical scholar. And in his effort to combine his philosophy with his love of the classics lies his chief fault as a student. If it be allowed that his theory of the liturgical origin of the drama is ingenious, it must also be granted that it owes much to classical analogues. The Greek drama grew out of antiphonal singing, which crept into the religious rites in honor of the wine-god Dionysus. "Both tragedy and comedy," says Aristotle, "originated in a rude and unpremeditated manner—the first from the leaders of the dithyramb, and the second from those who led off the phallic songs." [10] Magnin writes: "Things came to pass in the Middle Ages in the same manner as they did in antiquity. . . . The modern theater received, just as did that of antiquity, its first development in the ritual, hence it is necessary to subordinate in our researches the history of the aristocratic and popular drama to that of the ecclesiastical drama." [11] Nearly every critic since Magnin has borrowed this same dangerous analogy.[12]

[10] Adolphus W. Ward, "Drama," *Encyclopaedia Britannica,* 11th ed., Cambridge, University Press, 1910, Vol. VIII, pp. 475–546.

[11] *Origines* (ed. 1838) pp. xvi, xix.

[12] Monmerqué et Michel, p. iii, "En cela ils imitaient, sans s'en douter, les prêtes du paganisme, qui, dans les mêmes vues, avaient donné à l'art dramatique de l'antiquité ses premiers · developpements." Sepet, *Les Prophètes du Christ,* p. 2, "Le théâtre du moyen âge . . . suivant les mêmes lois que le théâtre antique était issu de le religion antique." It has been repeated countless times by popular writers. René Doumic, *Histoire de la littérature fran-*

Magnin himself may, or may not, have taken it directly
from Fontenelle. There is no direct evidence on this
point.[13]

Strangely enough, the French savant had not the con-
suming interest in the Middle Ages and the Gothic which
nourished Hugo, the artist. Indeed, he appears almost
languid in his approach to things medieval. Twice he attempted to write a history of "Les Origines du théâtre
moderne" (in 1838 and 1868); beginning both times with
the origins of the Greek theater, he brought his study down
to the fall of Rome, where it abruptly terminated. The
second time he labeled his work, "Les Origines du théâtre
antique et du théâtre moderne," but beyond the preface
he never mentioned the medieval stage. In so far as it is
possible to discover, neither ill-health nor pressing official
duties kept him from completing his task. The volume
which appeared was excellent; Magnin had the good sense
not to venture into a field in which he was obviously not
equipped. Perhaps he had no inclination to do so.

From a perusal of Magnin's contributions to journals,
one might be justified in assuming that the classical analogy
was his starting point and his whole theory. He merely announced an hypothesis, but offered no demonstration. The
remainder of his work, in so far as the medieval drama is

çaise, Paris, Delaplace, 1909, p. 61; Eduard Engel, *Geschichte der
englischen Literatur,* Leipzig, Bradstetter, 1915, p. 83: "Über den
Ursprung des Theaters im Mittelalter gilt jetzt als feststehend, dass
es ebendaher stammt, woher das Drama der Griechen entsprungen:
von gottesdienstlichen Bräuchen," etc.

[13] Bernard de Bovier de Fontenelle, *Oeuvres,* Amsterdam, 1764,
Vol. III, p. 2: "The origins of all things are nearly always hidden
from us . . . but happily we find here [in the theater] an origin for
poetry very near like that of the most ancient Greeks."

concerned,[14] was largely aesthetic criticism, but criticism of a high order. Immediately it becomes apparent that there are two things, neglected by Magnin, which should be undertaken by every serious student of the drama: (1) a study of the liturgical history of the Middle Ages to determine whether the liturgical theory is initially permissible in the light of the ritualistic development; (2) a comparative study of the tropes and the drama to determine precisely what relationships exist between the two. The development of the liturgy—"songs which haunt still the melancholy choirs"—is interesting enough in itself, even if it were not vital to our purpose, to invite our immediate attention. We turn to it here as logically the first step to be taken in our investigations.

[14] Exception to this statement might be made only with special reference to the miracle plays. Magnin noted the relation of these plays to the saints' legends, etc. Cf. *Journal des Savants* for 1860 (note 5, *supra*).

CHAPTER II

ANTIPHONAL SINGING AND THE MONASTIC CHURCH

OUR study of the liturgy takes us directly to the monastic church, for it was there, and not in the Church proper, that the tropes first appeared. I shall endeavor to show that this special liturgical development represents a distinct poetic movement which was primarily *lyrical*, rather than dramatic, and that, first coming into conflict with the new rimed poetry, and then with the drama, it was gradually corrupted by these forms and then disappeared almost completely.

We may first of all turn to the tropes. Their development, as I have remarked, was practically confined to the monastic church. Indeed the entire movement in monastic music and ritual has been called an "extra-liturgical development"[1] because it never became a part of the recognized liturgy of the true Church.[2] "Quelques églises les ont admis;" writes Léon Gautier of the tropes, "l'Eglise, non pas."[3] In France, where this movement

---

[1] Léon Gautier, [*Histoire de la poesie liturgique au moyen âge:*] *les tropes,* Paris, Picard, 1886, p. 138. Compare W. H. Frere, *The Winchester Troper* (London, Henry Bradshaw Society, 1894) p.v: "Tropers are to the rest [of liturgical books] rather in the relation of an abortion to a living organism."

[2] Frederick G. Haskins, "Easter," *The Catholic Encyclopedia,* Vol. V, p. 226 ff.

[3] Gautier, *op. cit.,* p. 138.

began, the liturgy of the national church had once been that of the Gallican rite,[4] a service filled with "ceremonial ornament, symbolic practices, ritual adornment."[5] But beginning early in the seventh century, the Gallican rite was displaced slowly and surely by that of Rome.[6] The final and complete triumph for the latter came during the reign of Charlemagne (768–814), who insisted that all the churches in the realm should adopt the Roman missal of Gregory the Great.[7] "But in the long and gradual supplanting of the Gallican rite, the Roman rite itself was affected by its rival, so that when it at last emerges as sole possessor, it is no longer the pure Roman rite, but has become the Gallicanized Roman use that we now follow."[8] This Gallicanized Roman use, which for the sake of convenience I shall call Roman hereafter, once established, underwent very slight changes. Charlemagne carried off and destroyed the Ordinary of the Mass belonging to the old rite, so that further incursions from that direction were speedily checked. Carefully guarded by the Holy See,[9] the Roman liturgy has remained inviolate since that early time.

Obviously, then, the diocesan church, with its forced

[4] Frederick E. Warren, "Liturgy," *Encyclopaedia Britannica,* Vol. XVI, p. 797.

[5] Adrian Fortesque, "Liturgy, Medieval," *Catholic Encyclopedia,* Vol. IX, p. 312.

[6] Henry Jenner, "Gallican Rite," *Catholic Encyclopedia,* Vol. VI, p. 357.

[7] Warren, *op. cit.*

[8] Fortesque, *Catholic Encyclopedia,* Vol. IX, p. 312.

[9] For example, not even sequences could be sung out of season. Cf. Peter Wagner, *Introduction to the Gregorian Melodies: A Handbook of Plainsong,* London, Plainsong and Medieval Music Society, 1904 (280 pp.), p. 241, note 2.

conformity to the practice of the basilica of St. Peter's, is not the place to look for decided innovations in the liturgy. But when the eventful ninth century opened there did exist in a flourishing condition a powerful institution not immediately subject to Papal dictation. This was the Benedictine order of monks. The basis for the law and ritual of the Benedictines, of course, is found in the little book, *The Rule of St. Benedict*, prepared for the order by its tolerant patron saint.[10]

The *Rule* was the only tie between the different monasteries. Each congregation was otherwise an entity, with its own government, its own ecclesiastical calendar, and its own music. This meant considerable freedom for the Benedictines. Some chapters were, of course, intolerant of innovation, while others welcomed it. Further, "as the *Rule* shows, though St. Benedict required obedience to his code of laws, he never intended to prohibit other customs and practices not at variance with it."[11] On the other hand, as I have intimated, too much must not be made of the tolerance of the Benedictines; monasticism is essentially ascetic, and the reactionary movements of the Cluniac, Cistercian, and other orders,[12] show that there always existed a large group of monks who favored a strict observance of the *Rule*. The comparative scarcity of surviving manuscripts indicates that the extra-liturgical development was not so far-reaching as it might have been had

[10] Benedictus, St., *The Rule of St. Benedict,* translated, with an introduction, by Cardinal F. A. Gasquet, London, Chatto & Windus, 1909, 130 pp.

[11] Gasquet, *op. cit.,* Intro., p. xx.

[12] The Cistercians, Carthusians, and Cluniacs would have none of the innovations in church music. Cf. Peter Wagner, *op. cit.,* p. 242.

the whole order freely welcomed change.[13]   Consequently,
I have spoken above of the *constant opposition,* even in
the monasteries, which all innovation in church music
faced.[14]

"The center of the monastic life, according to the *Rule,*
was unquestionably the liturgy." [15]   This liturgy is incorporated in the Benedictine Breviary (*Breviarium Monas-
ticum*).   "St. Benedict devotes thirteen chapters (xviii-xxx)
of the *Rule* to regulating the canonical hours for his monks,
and the Benedictine Breviary is the outcome of the regu-
lation.   It is used not only by the so-called Black Benedictines, but also by the Cistercians, Olivetians, and all
those orders that have the *Rule* of St. Benedict as their
basis.   The Benedictines are not at liberty to substitute
the Roman for the Monastic Breviary; by using the Roman
Breviary they would not satisfy their obligation of saying
the Divine Office." [16]   The importance of the Benedictine
liturgy was stressed at the foundation of the Cluniac order,

---

[13] Only about 225 examples of the Easter trope, the most popular
of all, survive to represent *five centuries* of practice in all the
churches of Europe.

[14] "We are informed by Simeon of Durham that about the year
1083 King William the Conqueror appointed Thurstan, a Norman,
abbot of Glastonbury.   Thurstan, despising the ancient Gregorian
chanting, which had been used in England since the 6th century,
attempted to introduce in its place a modern style of chanting
invented by William of Fecamp, a Norman.   The monks resisted
the innovations of their abbot, and a scene of violence and blood-
shed ensued, which was terminated by the king's sending Thurstan
back to Normandy."   William Palmer, *Origines Liturgicae,* 4th ed.,
London, Francis, 1845, 2 vols., Vol. I, p. 187.

[15] Gasquet, *op. cit.,* Intro., p. xxv.

[16] Edmond M. Obrecht, "Benedictine Rite," *Catholic Encyclopedia,*
Vol. XIII, p. 74.

although the church services were multiplied far beyond the canonical office planned by St. Benedict.[17]

We are now prepared to consider the conditions under which additions to this liturgy took place. What prompted the creation of the Easter trope, the famous *Quem quaeritis*, and others?

The only existing historical account of the development of the tropes appears to confirm my contention that they were created for lyrical expression. This account, moreover, has been tacitly accepted by those who hold the liturgical theory for the origin of the drama.[18]

Charlemagne, who, as we have seen, was active in establishing the Gregorian ritual in the French church, was anxious that other Roman excellences should be grafted on Gallican institutions. Accordingly he brought to France two Italian Musicians, Pierre and Romaine, to develop the church music. One of these masters was established at Metz and the other at St. Gall. Their gift to France was a new and complicated music which gave great variety to the church chants. In place of the simple *Alleluia*—itself a lyrical expression of jubilation—*sequentia* were developed; musical runs were given to the final *a* of the word, which was greatly prolonged. But before long, choir and cantor began to complain that these variations were too complicated to remember; that, although the music was excellent, it imposed insuperable difficulties.[19] What was to be done at this juncture?

[17] Edward C. Butler, "Cluny," *Encyclopaedia Britannica,* Vol. VI, p. 569.

[18] For example, Sir Edmund K. Chambers, *The Medieval Stage* (Oxford, Clarendon Press, 1903, 2 vols.), Vol. II, p. 7 ff., C. M. Gayley, *Plays of Our Forefathers* (New York, Duffield, 1907, 349 pp.), p. 18 ff., C. F. Tucker Brooke, *The Tudor Drama,* p. 2 ff., etc.

[19] Gautier, *Les Tropes,* p. 13 ff.

"It is from the North that the light comes," exclaims Léon Gautier:

One day (it was about the year 860) a stranger presented himself at the gate of the abbey of St. Gall and solicited there, in a humble voice, that hospitality which the Benedictine abbeys never refused. The stranger was himself a monk and carried a great book under his arm. When they asked him from whence he came, he replied, "I come from the Abbey of Jumièges, which has been devastated by the Normans. My book is an Antiphonary; behold.". . .

The monks of St. Gall welcomed the stranger and gave to his book a still better welcome; but suddenly they made exclamations of surprise. The *sequelae* of the Alleluia, those difficult jubilees, those complicated runs, were not sung, in the Antiphonary of Jumièges, in the same fashion as in the books of St. Gall. THEY WERE NOT SUNG WITHOUT WORDS and upon the last vowel *a* of the word Alleluia. No, no; over in Neustria, they had made a step in advance, a decisive step, for they had replaced the vowel *a* by words, by a tallying text, which had for its purpose the fixing in the memory of the complicated melodies of the alleluias. For each syllable there was a corresponding note; for each note a syllable. The whole formed a literary work grafted in a servile fashion on a musical work, but it was, and would become, a living thing! The great, the true memory method had finally been found, and it was that which excited the monks of St. Gall.[20]

There was a young novitiate at St. Gall, by the name of Balbulus Notker who, more than all the others, saw the possibilities of the sequences with words. "Notker found fault with the composition of these hymns—the syllables were not well placed—and set himself to supply words for the melodies according to a strict principle, giving a syllable to each note. *Psallat ecclesia mater illibata* was his first sequence, and this was followed by many more, until, in 887, a book of sequences was complete. But the ideas

[20] *Ibid.,* pp. 18, 19.

of St. Gall spread rapidly; all the world knew what was being done or thought in the great monastery. Almost before Notker was ready, the form of the sequence had established itself, and had even imposed itself on the vernacular French in the poem of St. Eulalia." [21]

Now this account is clear enough, and there seems small warrant in it for assuming that the purpose of the composers of the first tropes was to provide even a rudimentary form of drama. They appear to have been dissatisfied with the Alleluia chant as an expression of jubilation, and they elaborated that chant in a rather obvious fashion. Notker's *Psallat ecclesia mater illibata* is beyond dispute a lyric. Why are not the other pieces that were similarly inspired also lyrical? Why is not the *Quem quaeritis* lyrical? Why are not its offspring?

The fact that the tropes had their origin in the melismatic Alleluia, in that wordless lyrical chant of jubilation, should be linked with another fact which has apparently escaped the attention of those who assert that some of the tropes are dramatic. If the purpose of the composers of these pieces was to provide drama for Catholic congregations, it is hard to understand why the tropes were composed in Latin and not in some dialect more comprehensible to the people. As early as 812, within a few years of the creation of the *Quem quaeritis*, the bishops, meeting in council at Tours, decreed that, "since Latin was becoming ever less intelligible to the people, the homilies should be translated into the rustic language." [22] It is conceivable, perhaps, that the authors of the tropes should have chosen Latin for the first pieces, but that they should have re-

[21] W. P. Ker, *The Dark Ages*, New York, Scribners, 1904, p. 218 ff.
[22] J. Bédier et P. Hazard, *Histoire de la littérature française*, Larousse, Paris, 1923 (2 vols.), Vol. I, p. 4.

tained it for several centuries does not seem plausible—
that is, if the purpose of the composers was dramatic.

On the other hand, the choice of Latin is easily comprehensible if the intention of the composers was lyrical. So
far as the congregation was concerned, it merely continued
the tradition of the wordless sequences. Here was nothing
new or startling, save the more elaborate music one would
naturally expect on the festival days of the year. From
the standpoint of the singers, Latin was a normal choice
both for a memory device and for a statement of their
most exalted feelings.

Origin and language supply arguments, then, against the
theory that the trope normally developed into a dramatic
form. But in the fact that the tropes were performed only
on specific festival occasions resides a still graver objection. Well worth noting is the opinion of Geiger that
the lyrical is distinguished from the dramatic by its selection of the feeling of a particular moment or occasion,[23]
—just such an occasion as the special ritual of the fête
days would seem to provide. Have the advocates of the
liturgical theory demonstrated that, although the tropes
were given only on a stated festival and are always in
spirit with that festival, they have only an incidental connection with it? They have not. Instead, they have urged
us to believe that dramatic progress is most marked in
those tropes which belong, of all festivals, to the Easter
season! I maintain that the normal progress of a lyrical
rite, recited only on an occasion of great spiritual rejoicing, is in a lyrical direction. I believe that the burden
of proof is with those who think otherwise.

[23] The lyric deals with "the feeling of a particular moment or occasion, whereas the drama deals with a revolution of time and the
emotions appropriate thereto." (E. Geiger, *Beiträge zu einer
Aesthetik der Lyrik,* Halle, 1905).

We need to understand the trope even better, however, before we can study its progress. Gautier's definition is this: "LE TROPE EST L'INTERPOLATION D'UN TEXT LITURGIQUE: interpolation que l'on a principalement l'occasion de constater, depuis le IX° jusqu' au XII° siècle, dans certains livres de chant à l'usage des églises de l'Allemagne, de l'Italie, de la France." But to this he affixes a very important note: "Sauf de rares exceptions, *ces Eglises sont monastiques,* et c'est ce qu' a fort bien vu le Cardinal Bona en son beau livre que Martène appelle un Traité d'Or: *Rerum Liturgicarum, libri duo* (Rome, 1671, p. 296): 'Quorum troporum exstant exempla in antiquis monasteriorum libris. A monachis enim, private quorundam abbatum auctoritate, ut prisca ferebant tempora, haec additamenta originem traxisse puto, qui non solum introitus, sed alias etiam liturgicas preces eodem modo interpolarunt.' " [24]   So far as I know, this is the most extended notice anywhere of the important part which the monasteries played in the appearance and growth of the tropes.[25]   Most writers on the drama of this period speak vaguely of the trope originating in "the church," but it is very necessary that we insist that it originated in the Benedictine monastic church.   Thus Sir Edmund K. Chambers cannot understand why the *Quem quaeritis* is so rare in Italy and almost nonexistent in Spain.[26]   The answer seems to be that in Italy the Pope watched the liturgy too

[24] *Les Tropes,* p. 1, note 1. See also p. 73.

[25] William Maskell, however, implies the same point when he says of the tropes: "Certainly the monastic uses were more full of them than the diocesan." (*The Ancient Liturgy of the Church of England,* Oxford, Clarendon Press, 1882, 3 vols. Vol. I, p. 59.)

[26] *The Medieval Stage,* Oxford, Clarendon Press, 1903 (2 vols.), Vol. II, p. 35.

carefully,[27] while in Spain there were no Benedictine monasteries.[28]

Gautier's effort to prove that the verse of the early tropes was measured on a principle of assonance does not seem very conclusive.[29] More accurate, probably, is the following summary by W. P. Ker, who had occasion to review Gautier's work:

The sequences are not to be scanned according to any classical rule, nor yet by the methods accepted for the "rhythmical" poetry, as explained by Bede. They follow the melody exactly, and the tunes of that time were not in accordance with any of the known poetical measures, either classical or popular. In principle, the sequences are governed by the same general law as Pindar— namely, the words follow the music. But as the music was of a new kind, the words obeyed no established poetical law. Their measures are hard to understand with only the words to judge by. *One kind of regularity they indeed profess on the face of them. As the melody fell into periods, each of which repeated the same notes, the poetical sequence takes the form of a series of couplets or stanzas, each couplet or stanza having its own pattern.*[30]

Thus in the *Quem quaeritis* (see p. 2), we should judge that there are two periods represented, for the first and third lines are of twelve syllables each, while the second and fourth contain fifteen. The "o" which is so frequently

[27] "Progress in choral music was not possible in Italy, where the slightest deviation from the rules and traditions observed by the Roman singers was considered a sacrilege punishable with imprisonment." Arthur Mees, *Choirs and Choral Music*, London, Murray, 1901 (251 pp.), p. 33.

[28] E. C. Butler, "Monasticism," *Encyclopaedia Britannica*, Vol. XVIII, p. 687 ff.

[29] Gautier, *Les Tropes*, p. 157 ff.

[30] Ker, *The Dark Ages*, p. 220.

placed in the first line before *Christicolae* by many editors is redundant. It is not in the manuscript.[31]

Now if Ker was right about the dependence of the verse upon the melody—and all the early tropes which I have examined seem to bear him out—he has supplied us with additional evidence to buttress the historical argument that the tropes were lyrical. It is noteworthy, too, that no vestige of the type of versification found in the early tropes is discoverable in the fully developed drama. The verse of that drama, as we shall see, was modeled on Provençal forms.

Critics, like W. H. Frere, who have held that the St. Gall *Quem quaeritis* is in itself dramatic [32] have not only failed to observe how very dependent the verse is upon the melody, but they have also overlooked the fact that the assignment of parts in this trope is directly opposite from that which they must have supposed. This error probably comes from the assumption that the inquiry, "Quem quaeritis in sepulchro, Christicolae?" was sung by the cantor, while the *Responsio*, "Jesum Nazarenum crucifixum, o caelicolae," was sung by the choir. But the medieval *Respond* should not be confused with the congregational *response* in modern Protestant churches. The *Respond* was the most difficult musical part and was usually sung as a solo by the leader of the choir.[33] If it is

[31] St. Gall MS 484.

[32] The *Quem quaeritis* was "a dramatic dialogue which came to be used as a trope to the Introit of Easter," Frere, *The Winchester Troper*, p. xvi.

[33] "In all Latin liturgies . . . the responsorial chant is *richly developed melodically,* as is suitable for a soloist, while the antiphonal is simpler, more or less syllabic, as befits chants which are to be practicable for those who are not skilled singers. This contrast was so real in the Middle Ages that wherever in the MSS an A

held that the first inquiry was sung by a soloist representing the angel at the tomb, it is plainly a mistake, for this
chant is labeled *It* (an abbreviation standing for *Introit*,
which was always an antiphon [34]), while the second verse
is marked *R*, for *Respond*.[35] Any hypothesis that this
second verse (the solo or *Respond*) was a choral, and that
those who sang it represented the three Marys about to
visit the tomb of Christ, is, it would appear, untenable. In
the assignment of chants there is no evidence for the assumption of rôles on the part of the singers.[36]

But whoever would prove the *Quem quaeritis* dramatic,
must do more, as I have already pointed out, than show
that the parts were distributed as rôles. The identification
of an individual singer or reciter with a definite historical
or fictitious character is not unnatural to lyrical expression. It must be shown that this trope was something different from the other early tropes, that it was not an
amplified alleluia, an extended *jubilus* in words.

Now the *Quem quaeritis* was the *alleluia* sung as an
introductory antiphon to the Introit psalm. It might be
suggested that it came to take the place of this psalm, but
we cannot be certain of his point. All liturgists are agreed,
however, that the *Quem quaeritis* is but an embroidery or

(antiphon) is found marked at the beginning of a chant, a more
simple melody may be looked for; but a rich one wherever there
stands an R (respond)." Peter Wagner, *Handbook of Plainsong*,
p. 49.

[34] The Office of the Mass consists, in the first place, of *Antiphons*,
which are called *Introit* etc." Aurelian of Reome (ninth century)
Musica disciplina, ch. 20, quoted by Wagner, *Handbook of Plainsong*, p. 51.

[35] St. Gall MS 484, facsimile, Gautier, *Les Tropes*, p. 216.

[36] This discussion applies specifically to the earliest forms of the
Quem quaeritis.

extension of the Introit. It was sung after the choir was in position and while the choir and the congregation attended the entrance of the celebrant.[37] Considered as a decorative part of the Introit, the *Quem quaeritis* can hardly be regarded as dramatic. The "dramatic" thing is the entrance of the priest to celebrate the Mass, either while this *extended alleluia* was being sung or (in case of delay) immediately after. All in all, it would appear that there is scant justification for terming the St. Gall Easter trope "dramatic."

[37] Compare:

(a) "According to the liturgical writings of the Middle Ages, the Introit was performed in Rome, from the time of Gregory the Great onwards, as follows: when all the preparations for the Mass were finished and the candles were lit, the *Schola Cantorum*, the *Paraphonistae* and the boys placed themselves in two rows before the altar, according to their rank, and the chief of the singers, the *Prior Scholae*, intoned the antiphon to the Introit (that is, he gave the air for the psalm or the trope). At this moment the Pontiff, with his retinue, proceeded from the Sacristy into the Church. On arriving at the altar, and after adoring the Holy Host, he gave a sign to the *Prior Scholae* that he was to start the *Gloria* (at the end of the psalm). Bowing to the Pontiff, he obeyed his command. At the end of the *Sicut erat* the Pontiff went from the altar to his seat, and the whole concluded with the antiphon. This description in the *Ordo Romanus I* is clear, but may be supplemented by notes in the remaining *Ordines*, etc." Wagner, *op. cit.*, p. 57.

(b) "The Introit received its name from the approach of the priest to the altar." *Micrologus de ecclesiasticis observationibus*, Migne, *Patrolog. Lat.* Vol. CLI, col. 979.

(c) "Tropus proprie est quidam versiculus, qui in praecipius festivitatibus cantatur immediate *ante* introitum, *quasi quodam praeambulum, et continuatio ipsius introitus*." Durand, Tom. IV, cap. 5, quoted, Maskell, *The Ancient Liturgy etc.*, Vol. I, p. 28, note 26.

(d) Cf. various articles in the *Catholic Encyclopedia:* "Antiphon," "Antiphonary," "Choir," "Introit," "Mass," "Trope," etc.

Let us follow the history of the *Quem quaeritis* a bit further. Chambers writes:

This [the St. Gall] is the earliest and simplest form of the *Quem quaeritis*. It recurs, almost unaltered, in a tenth century troper from St. Martial of Limoges. In the eleventh century tropers it is a little more elaborate:

"*Tropus in Die*
Quem quaeritis in sepulchro, Christicolae?
Iesum Nazarenum crucifixum, o caelicolae.
Non est hic, surrexit sicut praedixerat;
Ite, nuntiate quia surrexit. Alleluia.
Ad sepulchrum residens angelus nuntiat resurrexisse Christum:
Et ecce completum est illud quod olim ipse per prophetam dixerat
    ad patrem taliter inquiens.
            Resurrexi"

Here the appended portion of the narrative makes the trope slightly less dramatic." [38]

But why does Chambers call these last two lines an "appended portion"? Why may they not be normal growth and development? As he admits, they are not dramatic. Why are they not an indication that there was some tendency on the part of the tropes away from the dramatic?

Unfortunately, there are no known St. Martial records which shed a distinct light upon the precise reason for the elaboration of the trope. But a number of causes which might have operated and which have been overlooked by those who hold the liturgical theory may be mentioned here. Why may not the growth, which ought to be considered primarily as an extension in music, have been due to an increase in religious fervor or an intensification of the lyrical spirit, just such a cause as was responsible for the appearance of the tropes themselves? In the second place, may there not have been a real necessity for amplifying this Introit as congregations grew larger and tardiness be-

[38] Chambers, *Medieval Stage*, Vol. II, p. 9.

came more frequent? [39] We know that in some cases the Introit was protracted by singing the psalm over and over again; why may not the monks at St. Martial's have solved this difficulty by expanding the trope? The prosaic quality of the added lines almost tempts one to adopt this point of view. Moreover, the Introit probably meant little to the congregation. [40] Why, then, may not the singers, faced with the task of supplying sound in the interval before the Mass, have lengthened the trope partly because they were interested in the music? Now a final, and more important query: If any one, or all, of these three causes affected the growth of this St. Martial *Quem quaeritis*, why may they not have operated to some extent throughout the history of the development of the tropes? That is,

---

[39] According to the *Musica disciplina*, persons were freely permitted to enter the church during the singing of the Introit (Cf. Wagner, *op. cit.*, p. 51): "In an old exposition of the Mass, the task of the Introit is thus stated: 'Quoniam animus ad multa divisus, tumultibus curarum saecularium perturbatur, et non statim, ut ecclesiam ingredimur, omnium huius sollicitudinum possumus oblivisci; quo purius et attentuis puriorem atque attentiorem orationem ad Dominum fundere videamur: quod Antiphona ad Introitum decantatur et suavi interposita . . . praeparatio est et exercitatio animorum: ut animus populi a mundanis cogitationibus, his omnibus paulatim avulsus, ad coelestia cogitanda ac desiderando trahatus.'" (Tomanasi, Vol. xii, praef. 4), quoted, Peter Wagner, *op. cit.*, p. 59, note 2. The Introit was a tumult-quelling office. Hence it became the approved custom "to fill up the time, till the beginning of the Mass proper, with chanting which might be longer or shorter, as was needed." Wagner, *op. cit.*, p. 59.

[40] "To the category of Chorals belong the Introitus, Offertorium, and . . . sequences (Prosa) sung by the choir. There developed also a large corpus of Latin hymns and antiphons. *Sung by the clergy and choir, they were as little intelligible to the passive congregation as the Mass itself.*" *Grove's Dictionary of Music and Musicians*, "Chorals."

do the tropes owe their growth to the "dramatic element" planted in the St. Gall Easter liturgy which proved "widely popular and rapidly extended itself," [41] or to other perfectly natural causes?

At any rate the first change in the trope in the extant documents—its first growth—is not toward the dramatic at all, but away from it. A second, and somewhat less common, change is its union with the symbolic ceremony of the *Elevatio Crucis* at dawn on Easter morning. Before we can appreciate the nature of this union, we must understand the significance of the ceremony to which the trope was joined. Professor Joseph Quincy Adams has reproduced the account of a sixteenth-century gentleman who witnessed the rites of the *Elevatio Crucis* in the Monastic Church of Durham:

There was in the Abbye Church of Duresme verye solemne service uppon Easter Day, betweene three and four of the clocke in the morninge, in honour of the RESURRECTION, where two of the oldest Monkes of the Quire came to the Sepulchre, being sett upp Good Friday, after the Passion, all covered with red velvett and embrodered with gold, and then did sence it, either Monke with a pair of silver sencers sittinge on theire knees before the Sepulchre. Then they both rising come to the Sepulchre, out of which, with great devotion and reverence, they tooke a marvelous beautifull *Image of our Saviour*, representing the resurrection, with a crosse in his hand, in the brest wherof was enclosed in bright christall the holy Sacrament of the Altar, throughe which Christall the Blessed Host was conspicuous to the behoulders. Then, after the elevation of the said picture, carryed by the said two Monkes uppon a faire velvett cushion, all embrodered, singinge the anthem of *Christus resurgens*, they brought it to the High Altar, and senceing it all the while that the rest of the whole quire was singinge the fore-said anthem of *Christus resurgens*, etc.[42]

[41] Tucker Brooke, *The Tudor Drama*, p. 2.
[42] *Chief Pre-Shakesperean Dramas*, Boston, Houghton Mifflin,

Strange as it may seem, Professor Adams prints this account of the *Elevatio Crucis* as dramatic material. But have we genuine imitative action described here? Did the visitor to Durham Cathedral see anything which might be described as dramatic gesture, mimicry, or pose on the part of the celebrants? In his own words, it was a "verye solemne service." The word *solemn* means fundamentally something "full of ceremony," which would seem to apply far better to the liturgy, as in the term *missa solemnis*, than to the drama.

In evidence of the contention that ritualistic ceremony need not be dramatic in character I wish to reproduce the following account of the Sarum Processional for Easter Day. Though this account must be well known to everyone who has examined the liturgy, it has never been printed as the report of a dramatic performance. Yet it will be perceived at once that the ceremony therein described was very like the Durham rite.

The Sarum Processional

On Easter Day before Mass and the ringing of the bells, the clerks shall assemble at the church, and all the lights shall be lit throughout the church. Two clerks of higher rank, with candle bearers, thurifers, and the clergy around them, shall go to the sepulchre, and after first sencing the sepulchre with great veneration, that is to say, with genuflexion, they shall speedily and with privacy place the body of the Lord upon the altar. Then they shall take again the cross out of the sepulchre, and some person of superior rank shall begin the anthem, *Christ being raised, etc.* Therewith the procession shall advance by the South door of the presbytery through the middle of the quire. The cross, which has been raised from the sepulchre, is to be reverently borne on their

1924, p. 4. (Note especially the manner in which the anthem is sung, first by the two leaders, and then by the full choir.)

arms by the two priests aforesaid, with the thurifers and candle bearers preceding them, through the North door of the presbytery, to an altar on the North side of the church, those of higher rank advancing first, and the quire not changing their dress. The Lord's body, which has been placed in a pyx on the altar, shall be left in the custody of the sub-treasurer, who shall suspend it in the aforesaid pyx within the tabernacle. Then all the bells shall be rung in a clash and this anthem be sung: *Christ being risen from the dead dyeth no more; for in that he liveth, he liveth unto God. Alleluia, Alleluia!* [43]

The rite of the *Elevatio Crucis* of Durham and the Sarum *Processional* occupy a position identical with the St. Gall *Quem quaeritis,* that is, they are both extra-liturgical ceremonies preceding the Mass. We have seen that there is some probability that the *Quem quaeritis* may owe its origin to an intensification of the religious and lyrical emotion aroused by Easter Day. Certainly this spirit animates these kindred rites, each of which aspires to a climax in song. That this emotion, for which music had hitherto apparently provided an adequate expression, should here, in the *Elevatio Crucis* and the *Processional,* demand some outlet in action, is not incomprehensible. The theoretical repressions of the Lenten season coupled with the emotional release of Easter might lead naturally to joining action to feeling. As long as we lack direct evidence on the point, I shall believe that the growth of the Easter ceremonies in the ancient church was due to some such cause as this, rather than to a deliberate attempt to represent Biblical story.

The *Elevatio Crucis* and the *Processional* seem still

[43] *The Sarum Missal in English* trans. by Frederick E. Warren (The Library of Liturgiology and Ecclesiology for English Readers, ed. by Vernon Straley, VIII, IX), London, 1911 (2 vols.), Vol. II, p. 288.

to have been inadequate to express the rejoicing of the Easter season. Ever preoccupied with their liturgy, as the injunction of St. Benedict bade them be, certain monks must have comprehended this inadequacy. The chief interest of the liturgy was, of course, the music. Yet in both the *Elevatio* and the *Processional* the only music was the anthem, *Christus resurgens.* Moreover, whatever joy was expressed by this anthem was more than offset by the solemn *quête* and silent (even secret) removal of the Host —features of the service which partook of the prior Lenten season. Finally, human frailty made it inevitable that there should be constant late comers to this service at dawn who brought confusion to the church and annoyance to the celebrants. What would be more natural, then, than to move the *Elevatio Crucis* to the end of the service, after the lessons, and join to it the *Quem quaeritis* and other chants? This step, at any rate, represents the second change in the presentation of the Easter trope.

Evidence for this change is contained in the *Regularis Concordia* of St. Ethelwold (ca. 980), prepared for Winchester Cathedral. But as the rite therein described is concluded by the singing of the *Te Deum laudamus,* which apparently was not known in England prior to the Conquest,[44] it is highly likely that this rite is a later insertion by some monk who wished to give it the authority of St. Ethelwold. The dating of the Winchester *Sepulchrum,* as it is called, towards the end of the eleventh century is thoroughly in keeping with the changes which we have described. That is, if the *Quem quaeritis* originated about 890, and the *Elevatio Crucis* about the middle of the

[44] The earliest other known use of the *Te Deum* is in the Salisbury Breviary, where it was introduced by St. Osmund, about 1085. Cf. John Bumpus, *A Dictionary of Ecclesiastical Terms,* "Te Deum."

eleventh century,[45] the rite derived from these must be later still. It will appear, moreover, again and again in this study that the development of such rites as these, particularly in the beginning, was slow and cautious.

Far more important than the date of the *Sepulchrum* is the question of its character. Has the union of two pieces, undramatic in themselves, given rise to a service which may be considered dramatic? Sir Edmund K. Chambers is positive that it has. "The liberal *scenario* of the *Concordia Regularis*," he affirms, "makes plain the change which has come about in the character of the *Quem quaeritis*. . . . Dialogued chant and mimetic action have come together and the first liturgical drama is, in all its essentials, complete."[46] But Chambers does not give evidence for this statement, and we must judge for ourselves by turning directly to the account of the *Sepulchrum*. I reproduce the admirable translation, with the songs expanded from the cues, by Professor Adams:

While the third lesson is being chanted, let four brethren vest themselves; of whom let one, vested in an alb, enter as if to take part in the service, and let him without being observed, approach the place of the sepulchre, and there, holding a palm in his hand, let him sit down quietly. While the third responsory is being sung, let the remaining three follow, all of them vested in copes, and carrying in their hands censers filled with incense; and slowly, in the manner of seeking something, let them come before the place of the sepulchre. These things are done in imitation of the angel seated in the monument, and of the women coming with spices to anoint the body of Jesus. When therefore that one

[45] The earliest pure *Elevatio* is that published by Adams. But the *Processional* to which I have called attention is essentially the same rite. It may be dated about the year 1085. I doubt, however, if it is the first rite of this sort, though it may be. It is noteworthy that all the illustrations of the *Elevatio* thus far produced are English.

[46] *The Medieval Stage*, Vol. II, p. 15.

seated shall see the three, as if straying about and seeking something, approach him, let him begin in a dulcet voice of medium pitch to sing:

Whom seek ye in the sepulchre, O followers of Christ?

When he has sung this to the end, let the three respond in unison:

Jesus Nazareth, which was crucified, O celestial one.

To whom that one:

He is not here; he is risen, just as he foretold,
Go, announce that he is risen from the dead.

At the word of this command, let those three turn themselves toward the choir saying:

Alleluia!   The Lord is risen today,
The strong lion, the Christ, the Son of God!

This said, let the former, again seating himself, as if recalling them, sing the anthem:

Come, and see the place where the Lord was laid!
Alleluia! Alleluia!

And saying this, let him rise, and lift the veil, and show them the place bare of the cross, but only the cloths laid there with which the cross was wrapped. Seeing which, let them set down the censers which they carried into the same sepulchre, and let them take up the cloth *and spread it out before the eyes of the clergy;* and, as if making known that the Lord had risen and was not now therein wrapped, let them sing this anthem:

The Lord is risen from the sepulchre
Who for us was hung on the cross.

And let them place the cloth upon the altar. The anthem being ended, let the Prior, rejoicing with them at the triumph of our King, in that, having conquered death, he arose, begin the hymn:

We praise thee, O God!

This begun, all the bells chime out together.[47]

Generally critics have concurred with Chambers that

[47] Adams, *op. cit.,* pp. 9, 10.

this *"scenario"* is dramatic, that it contains dialogue and mimetic action. They are apparently agreed that, in the performance of the *Sepulchrum,* Biblical story was actually represented by speech and gesture.[48] And this in spite of the fact that it would have been extraordinary indeed had there been many persons in the nave who understood even the language of the chants!

In the second place, is it at all possible to prove that the action suggested by the directions for performing the rite is dramatic in character? Why is this action not the appropriate accompaniment, as in the Mass, with the priest at the altar, to lyrical and religious emotion? Indeed, is not the balance of probability in favor of a lyrical, rather than a dramatic, interpretation, since the history of the tropes, as we have followed it thus far, is lyrical?

Furthermore, it must not be forgotten that what we have examined is not the actual rite, but directions for performing the rite. Thus the direction to the monks to approach the sepulchre "as if seeking something" may well be understood as informing them of the precise nature of their part in the symbolical ceremony rather than instructing them in the art of histrionic representation. If one were to become acquainted for the first time with the Mass by reading the *Ordinary,* one might think that Office far more "dramatic" than it actually is.

Nevertheless there are important features of this account which should not be overlooked. These would seem to furnish some positive evidence that the celebrants performing the rite were not especially concerned as to the effect of their mimetic abilities upon the congregation. Thus when the three brethren are instructed to announce that Christ is risen, they turn to the choir and the presby-

---

[48] Compare Gayley, *op. cit.,* p. 15; Tucker Brooke, *op. cit.,* p. 3, etc.

tery, with their backs to the congregation, to sing the anthem. Again, when they take up the cloths in which the cross was wrapped, it is to the clergy that they are instructed to display them. But these brethren are themselves celebrants, for they take part in the singing of the *Te Deum laudamus* at the climax of the rite.[49] If, then, the effect of the dialogue was lost upon the congregation because of the language in which it was written, and if the effect of the action is likewise susceptible of challenge, ought we assume, on the basis of the *Concordia Regularis* account alone, that in the Winchester *Sepulchrum* "the first liturgical drama is, in all its essentials, complete"?

Viewed from still another angle, it would appear that the composer had moved the rite from the beginning of the service for liturgical, rather than dramatic, effect. Is not the aim of the piece to progress from antiphonal singing to concerted rejoicing? In other words, is not the end sought an exaltation of the spirit through symbolism to an emotional outpouring which shall involve all the singers, the Prior, the choir, and the clergy? Note how the action tends away from the dramatic, until finally the brother representing the angel and the brethren representing the Marys join in the same symbolic movement, for the benefit of the clergy,[50] to indicate the Resurrection of Christ. What a fitting emotional and lyrical climax the piece now provides for the Easter service! Considering the conditions under which it was presented, it is impossible to as-

[49] The congregation did not even take part in the singing of the *Te Deum* in medieval times. Cf. Wagner, *Handbook of Plainsong*, p. 151.

[50] Nothing could more plainly indicate the ritualistic nature of the piece and the indifference of the composer for the congregation than the phrase, *Sumantque linteum et extendant contra clerum, ac veluti ostendentes quod surrexit Dominus.*

sume that the Winchester *Sepulchrum* is more dramatic
than its progenitor, the *Quem quaeritis* of St. Gall. The
English *Sepulchrum* has more ornament, more symbolism,
but the greatest advance has been toward the lyrical. The
Sepulchrum is merely a more extended *jubilus*—the proper
heir of the wordless sequences, the melismatic alleluias of
the ninth century. This growing lyrical trend in the
Easter liturgy, which, as is well known, ultimately gave
rise to religious lyrics, has been entirely ignored by the
school of critics of whom Charles Magnin was the first
exponent. The perfectly natural and essentially *lyrical
Te Deum* climax, with its exultant clash of bells, will have
to be explained away before we can see significant dramatic growth or evolution going on in the liturgy.

On two counts, then, we may dismiss the theory that the
Winchester *Sepulchrum* is dramatic in its nature: (1) it is
derived from rites which are lyrical, and (2) in actual presentation, in so far as we are justified in making an assumption, it was primarily lyrical. On the basis of our
reëxamination of the documentary evidence which has been
offered, the *Quem quaeritis* of St. Gall, the *Quem quaeritis*
of the eleventh century tropers, and the account of the
Winchester *Sepulchrum* contained in the *Concordia Regularis*, we may doubt not only that these pieces are dramatic, but also that it has been established that there is
any tendency in their growth toward the dramatic. It is
consistent with the general history of the liturgy to suppose
that all that these composers were aiming to produce was a
lyrical and religious effect.

A detailed study of the other pieces which illustrate the
natural development of this Easter rite throughout the later
centuries of its use can really bring nothing pertinent to our
problem of origins. If the reader will turn, however, to

the *Office of the Resurrection* celebrated in the monastic church of Kloster-Neubourg, in Germany, from the thirteenth to the sixteenth centuries,[51] he will discover therein a comparatively representative piece, more elaborate than the Winchester *Sepulchrum*, but apparently no more dramatic. He will observe that the important parts in the *Office* are assigned, as in the celebration of the Mass, to the higher clergy, evidently without regard to their histrionic ability. Thus *Prelatus* leads the procession to remove the cross from the sepulchre, *Presbyteri* take the "parts" of the Marys and of John and Peter, while the "rôle" of the Angel is assigned specifically to *Diaconus!* [52] If the *clerici* had any part in this ceremony, it was as undistinguished members of the choir. Nothing could be clearer than the composer's intention to dignify his ceremony by placing it in worthy hands.[53] Furthermore, the same lyrical progress toward an emotional climax is observable in this rite as in the Winchester *Sepulchrum*. Thus the Prior and those accompanying him, having removed the Crucifix in a devout and reverent manner, softly take up the chant, *Surrexit pastor bonus*. The fashion of singing this (*ac canentis sub silentio*) may be compared with the saying of the private prayer in the Mass today. It is a rite wholly for the chief communicant and his immediate group. But the succeeding chants involve larger

[51] Printed in Edéléstand DuMéril, *Origines latines du théâtre moderne,* Paris, 1849, p. 89 ff.

[52] I use the terms "parts" and "rôle" only for convenience, not to attach any dramatic quality to the chants thus designated.

[53] A glance back at the texts of the *Elevatio Crucis* and of the Sarum *Processional* show that the more dignified of the clergy took part in these rites. That the Winchester *Sepulchrum* was likewise performed by the elder ecclesiastics, is an obvious inference.

and larger numbers of singers, until all the clergy join in
singing the *Te Deum laudamus.*

If we were to examine the Christmas and the Ascension
tropes, we should observe that their chief characteristics
are symbolical and lyrical, rather than dramatic. For
example, in the following translation of the St. Gall Christmas trope, notice that two of the singers are concealed,
that the rite is ostensibly performed in the choir, that the
important rôles are taken by the deacons, and that there is
definite progress in the rite to a lyrical climax:

On Christmas day let two deacons be prepared, clad in dal-
matics, and behind the altar let them say:
"Whom seek ye in the manger, Shepherds, say?"

Let two choir-boys reply:
*"The Saviour, Christ the Lord, a babe wrapped in swaddling
clothes, according to the word of the Angel."*

Then the deacons:
*"The child is here, with Mary his mother, concerning whom in
prophecy Isaiah foretold: Lo, a Virgin shall conceive and bring
forth a Son. Now, proclaiming, tell that He is born."*

Then the Cantor shall say in a shrill voice:
*"Alleluia, alleluia. Now we know in truth that Christ is born
on earth; of whom, sing all ye, saying with the prophet, Christ is
born."*

The reader must never forget that these distant, mystical
rites, performed wholly by the clergy, were not meant for
the layman's head but for his heart. Symbolic rites, growing naturally out of the melismatic Alleluia, the *jubilus,*
were not necessarily understood even by the performers.
As St. Augustine says, in his exposition of the Ninty-ninth
Psalm, "He who sings a *jubilus,* speaks no words, but it
is a song of joy without words; it is the voice of a heart
dissolved in joy, which tries as far as possible to express

the feeling, even if it does not understand the meaning." [54]
For the reader who is familiar with the Church ritual of
today, a distinct light is shed on the non-dramatic nature
of the bulk of the tropes by the fact that the *Kyrie*,
Sanctus, and *Agnus*, essentially lyrical pieces, alone survive.[55]

[54] Wagner, *Handbook of Plainsong*, p. 32.
[55] Cf. Gautier, *Les Tropes*, p. 155 ff.

Chapter III

THE CONTAMINATION OF THE LITURGY

If, as I maintain, the *Quem quaeritis* is not dramatic and the rites that have naturally grown from it are not primarily dramatic, there is no question that there survive in manuscript form tropes and pseudotropes which are appreciably dramatic. Furthermore, it is possible that in the decline of interest in the liturgy many a sacred rite was celebrated in a manner not far removed from the theatrical. It was probably observation of these facts which led Magnin to conclude that the mystery plays were derived from the liturgy. But a more careful scrutiny of the texts would, perhaps, have led him to the conclusion that *this dramatic element was not the result of growth but of contamination.* First, he would have observed that the dramatic elements are suspicious from a liturgical standpoint, that is, they are not normal additions to the tropes under discussion; secondly, that the texts so corrupted are all comparatively late. Assuming for the moment that these elements were introduced from without at a late date, the question naturally arises: May not this corruption in the liturgy come from the drama itself? That is, may not the relationships between the drama and the liturgy be precisely the reverse of what has been claimed?

That the tropes were, as an extra-liturgical development unsanctioned by authority, subject to contamination is antecedently probable. Furthermore the point is capable

37

of some demonstration. We have seen that the trope appeared with a system of versification peculiar to itself, derived from the complicated chant on which the words w~re based. In some cases, notably in the development which we have just traced from the St. Gall *Quem quaeritis* to the rite celebrated at Kloster-Neubourg, this verse form remained essentially unchanged. But the movement as a whole suffered a different fortune. No better summary of the facts may be found than that of M. Gautier:

> The first tropes, as we have shown already, belong without doubt to the end of the ninth century or the beginning of the tenth. Their diffusion was rapid, and does not seem to have ceased throughout the course of the tenth century. We designate what we dare to call their glory as falling in the first half of the eleventh century; certainly their decadence commenced at the end of the same century. In the twelfth century, the new tropes, the Rimed-Tropes, *les Tropes-motets, les Tropes-chansons* became little by little all the fashion; but in the fourteenth century the whole lot disappeared together, save some choice pieces which resisted the weather. Such are the very ancient tropes of the *Kyrie*, the *Sanctus*, and the *Agnus*, which we find in the Roman Missal of Paul III and in other Missals still more modern. That is all.[1]

The first tropes flourished, then, till toward the end of the eleventh century, at which point they began to falter before the attacks of a new kind of trope, the rimed trope, which steadily displaced them. It was plainly a test of strength in which rime conquered. Gautier believed that the new tropes appeared between 1070 and 1080. He was able to date the change thus exactly from a similar change in verses to commemorate the passing of monks in a certain monastery. These death lists dated the demise of

[1] *Op. cit.,* p. 81.

each monk therein celebrated.[2] While M. Gautier does not appear to have considered the possibility that the epitaphs of this community may have been brought up to date many years after the deaths which they record, his dating is approximate enough to serve any purpose of ours.

After examining a considerable number of the new or rimed tropes, I have come to the conclusion that a strong influence was exerted upon them by the verse forms of the troubadours. For example, this trope which Gautier prints as an illustration of the *Proses* of the second period,[3] is in a stanza form used by Bertrand de Born:

> Qui procedis ab utroque,
> Genitore, Genitoque,
> Pariter, Paraclite,
> Redde linguas eloquentes,
> Fac ferventes in te mentes
> Flamma tua divite.[4]

Setting aside for the moment the question whether the piece known as *Les Vierges Sages et Les Vierges Folles* is a genuine trope or a mere imitation, its stanzas (of which the following are an illustration), written in the Provençal verse forms and dialect, are eloquent proof of troubadour influence and possibly of troubadour composition:

> Oiet, virgines, aiso que vos dirum,
> Aiset presen, que vos comandarum:
> Atendet un espos, Jhesu Salvaire a nom.
>   Gaire no i dormet
> Aisel espos que nos hor'atendet.
>
> Venet en terra per los vostres pechet,
> De la Virgine en Betleem fo net,

[2] *Ibid.,* p. 155 ff.

[3] *Ibid.,* p. 157.

[4] Compare F. W. Maus, *Peire Cardenals Strophenbau,* Marburg, Elvertische, 1884, p. 87.

E flum Jorda lavet et luteet.
Gaire no i dormet
Aisel espos que nos hor'atendet.[5]

While all the stanzas used in the new tropes do not correspond as closely as these to the poetry of the troubadours,
there is a general similarity which cannot be denied.[6] All
the devices of troubadour versification are there: balance,
internal rime, refrain, play upon words. Moreover, the
very variety of the new stanza forms in the liturgy suggests a troubadour influence. Consequently I have come
to the conclusion that the tropes were in many cases as
closely imitated from the verse of the minstrels as caution
and the music of the church would permit.

Confirmatory of this influence of the minstrels upon the
liturgy is the fact that the ancient Tropers contain por-
traits of minstrels and entertainers. Léon Gautier reproduced some of these (on pages 106, 107, and 125 of his
study), although he made no point of their presence there.
It is significant that the change in trope form came when
the troubadours were just beginning to exert an influence
upon poetry.[7] There are two explanations, both of which
may be valid, of how these tropes came to be corrupted by
lay stanza forms and by rime. It may be that the liturgi-
ologists welcomed the new metrical devices because of their
popularity and novelty. That is a facile and, maybe, an

[5] Text and discussion, Monmerqué et Michel, *op. cit.*, p. 3 ff.

[6] I do not deny the influence which the Latin hymn may have
had upon the tropes. See the paragraph relative to this matter at
the close of this section of the discussion, p. 49.

[7] That is, at the beginning of the twelfth century. I have accepted the dates 1070–80 as only roughly approximate. Gautier has
produced no tropes of a date so early as this, and I have pointed
out that dating by the epitaphs of this community is at least
hazardous.

adequate, explanation. Yet it ignores the recognized liturgical tendency to preserve as sacred the forms which had become traditional. That tendency accounts for the very little difference (all things considered) in the actual celebration of the Winchester *Sepulchrum* and the *Office of the Resurrection* of Kloster-Neubourg, separated by several centuries from each other. A much better explanation, then, is that these new rimes were composed by persons who had the best reasons in the world for composing them, namely, the minstrels themselves. They had no reason to venerate liturgical custom. It is a notable fact that the twelfth century witnessed a tremendous decline of interest on the part of the ecclesiastics in their liturgy,[8] and particularly in these extra-liturgical practices.[9] Furthermore, it is well known that lay-canons were hired at this time to replace the vicars-choral, and even the praecentors, in the choir. So general had become this practice and the attendant evils that in 1233 we find a papal instruction prohibiting secular canons from entering the stalls of the choir, except in case of extreme necessity.[10] Now among these secular canons hired by the ecclesiastics were probably many jongleurs. They were from habit loiterers about the monasteries; their musical talents adequately equipped them for such occupations. They were possibly

---

[8] The ascetic and reactionary movements of the Cistercians, Carthusians, and of small orders in Italy (notably, that of Grammont) testify to the need at this time of reform in all spiritual matters.

[9] "In the twelfth century not only was the tide of feeling turning against the tropes, but ecclesiastical authority was being directed toward their suppression." W. H. Frere, *The Winchester Troper,* p. xiv.

[10] "Inhibemus ne aliquid saeculi canonici stallum in choro, etc." Andre Duschene, *Historiae Francorum Scriptores,* Paris, 1649. Vol. V, p. 818.

the first to violate the traditions of the choir, the first to introduce secular verses into the liturgy. When the fat monk came to care more for following his hounds than for following the airs of his monastic music,[11] when he entrusted his gold-lettered brevaries to laymen, corruption entered into his ritual. What might not these roguish substitutes in the choir do with the sacred *jubilus?*

If the minstrels had a share in this first corruption of the liturgy by rimed songs, is it not likely that they were responsible for the further degradation of the ritual by acting? Accustomed as these fellows were to making their livelihood by mimetic abilities, the temptation to present the liturgy by dramatic gesture could hardly have been resisted. Supplied with half a knowledge of things theological, ecclesiastical, and liturgical,[12] they were capable of producing just such ritualistic monstrosities as are some of the fugitive pieces with which a student of the liturgy must deal. It is significant that none of these pieces, examples of which I am about to offer, has been found in the regular choir books: they have been collected from dubious brevaries and miscellaneous manuscripts. The plain inference is that their performance depended upon

[11] There exists in the British Museum MS Arundel 292,f71b, a very amusing complaint of two monks, Dawn Watere and William, upon the difficulty of learning church music. They cannot even manage the *lectiones:*

> *"Qwan i kan un lesson to my master wil i gon*
> *That heres me in recital; he wennes i have wel don."*

[12] I am prepared to show that many minstrels must have been trained in the monastic schools. The outer schools were open to all who could afford it; the inner schools were free to the probationers. Note that the minstrel author of the *"Bible" of St. Denis* (which I quote below, p. 136) affirms that he has learned his narratives *in school.* Many other statements of this sort could be cited.

opportunity, when authority's back was turned. Their first appearance is in the twelfth century, as very occasional surreptitious practices substituted for the extra-liturgical rites of the church.

An examination of these pieces again provides a refutation of the theories of Magnin and indicates that the drama did not develop out of the liturgy, but forced its way into the extra-liturgical rites through the instrumentality of the professional actors of the day, the minstrels. Again I have not space enough to include all the evidence. But first let us consider the plays of Hilarius.

This man was a *scholaris vagans*, and it would be doing him no injustice, says Chambers, to call him a Goliard.[13] To judge from his verse, which is contained in a single manuscript,[14] he made his living, along with a few companions, in the earlier twelfth century, by minstrelsy. He is the author of jocund and amorous Latin verses of the Goliardic type and of short plays. His dramatic pieces are three in number: a long play wholly in Latin founded on the story of Daniel, and two shorter plays, in which the Latin lines are interspersed with a few lines in French, one based on a miracle wrought by St. Nicholas, the other on the raising of Lazarus. These pieces are totally unlike any of the extra-liturgical rites which have their origin in the Easter trope. They are in dialogue, tell a story for the story's sake, and are capable of being acted. Yet they pretend, *despite the fact that there is no obvious place in the church or monastic calendar for them*,[15] to be liturgical

---

[13] *Medieval Stage*, Vol. II, p. 57.

[14] Biblio. Nat. MS 11,331; edited as *Hilarii Versus et Ludi* by J. B. Fuller, New York, Holt, 1929, 129 pp.

[15] The St. Nicholas play might have been given, of course, on St. Nicholas' fête day, Dec. 6. I give Hilarius credit, however, for

pieces. At the end, both of the *Daniel* and of the *Suscitatio Lazari,* is a rubric or stage direction, to the effect that, if the performance is given at Matins, the *Te Deum* should follow; if at Vespers, the *Magnificat.*[16] This is little short of astonishing. Here are some plays, apparently not written for any church in particular and certainly composed without any regard whatever for the liturgy, which the author intends to introduce into the most important part of either the morning or evening service at any time in the year. Were they ever presented? There exists not a particle of evidence on this point. If we assume, as those who have followed Magnin generally have assumed, that these plays were actually given,[17] we cannot escape the conclusion that they furnish proof that the drama influenced the extra-liturgical rites, and not the converse.[18] Certainly the plays of Hilarius never could have developed out of the liturgy, especially at this early date.[19] But unquestionably influ-

originating something which could be turned to profit oftener than once a year.

[16] Chambers, *op. cit.,* Vol. II, p. 59.

[17] I believe we should be cautious in assuming this. The breviaries which not infrequently contain plays of this type were first of all introduced as little books to be taken on a journey for the private observance of the offices. (Cf. Mgr. Pierre Battifol, *History of the Roman Breviary* trans. by A.M.Y. Balay from the 3d French ed. London, Longmans, 1912 [333 pp.], p. 157.) If the "plays" were by any chance prepared for private consumption, ought they not be regarded as "closet dramas"?

[18] "I take it that these plays were not written for any church in particular, but represent the repertory of a band of wandering clerks. . . . As to the place of these plays in the calendar, the MS gives no indication, and probably Hilarius and his friends would be willing enough to act them whenever they got a chance." Chambers, *op. cit.,* Vol. II, p. 59.

[19] See below (page 81) for a discussion of the relationship of this play to the Arles *lectio* discovered by Sepet.

enced by him is the Beauvais *Daniel,* a late semi-dramatic
liturgical rite with many parallels to Hilarius, *perhaps*
annually performed as a prophecy in the service.[20]

Or let us examine the play, *Les Vierges Sages et Les
Vierges Folles.*[21] This piece dates from about the time of
Hilarius, but its author is unknown. The reader who is
familiar with the play will readily agree with me that it is
remarkably good. Had the author perhaps some training
as a playwright? While the piece does not contain dialogue (in the strictest sense), it at least contains chants
in character by different personages: Christus, Fatuae,
Prudentes, Mercatores; and there is a direction at its close
for the foolish virgins to be driven off to hell. But its
author, while a man of talent, was no liturgist. Had he
been, he never would have violated the Scriptures by making the narrator of the parable, Christ, the bridegroom.
This is, however, an artistic innovation of considerable
merit.[22] Furthermore, there never was an occasion in the
calendar for a rite with this as its theme. *Les Vierges
Sages et Les Vierges Folles,* if presented in the church services at all, must have gained that distinction by its merits
rather than by its connection with the liturgy. It is a further bit of proof that the liturgy became dramatic through
outside influences.

There is the greatest probability that the author of this
piece, prior to becoming a member of a monastic choir
(possibly that of Limoges, to the monastery of which the
MS once belonged), had been a jongleur or had come

[20] Cf. Marius Sepet, *Les Prophètes du Christ,* pp. 51, 52. Text in
Coussemaker, *op. cit.,* p. 49 ff.

[21] Biblio. Nat. MS 1139, f. 53. Printed, with the music, C.E.H.
Coussemaker, *Drames liturgiques du Moyen Age,* Paris, 1860, p. 1
ff. Text only, in DuMéril, *Origines latines,* p. 233 ff.

[22] Cf. Matt. 25:13.

under the influence of the jongleurs. Evidence for this is contained not only in the form and language of the verses which comprise the songs of the virgins, but also in the Latin stanzas at the beginning and end of the play. The reader should examine these in the text of Coussemaker, where the music is also given, since it, as well as the stanza form, is certainly of troubadour origin.[23]   Never are the musical phrases alternately repeated, as in the Gregorian chant, but there is that type of repetition found only in

[23] The printing of the first stanzas of this piece has given a good deal of difficulty to various editors, who, by concealing the true stanza form, have also hidden the character of the music. The last stanza in the piece (*modo veniat sponsus*) furnishes us with the true pattern:

> Amen dico
> Vos ignosco
> Nam carets lumine
> Quod qui pergunt
> procul pergunt
> Huius aule limine.

Hence the first verses should be printed in this fashion:

> Adest sponsus
> Qui est Christus
> vigilate, virgines!
> Pro adventu
> ejus gaudent
> et gaudebunt homines.
> (Air repeated):
> Venit enim
> liberare
> gentium origines,
> Quas per primam
> sibi matrem
> subjugarunt demones. etc.

Provençal compositions. The air is repeated from stanza to stanza, a novelty up to this time in trope music.[24]

If it be granted that in plays like those of Hilarius and like *Les Vierges Sages et Les Vierges Folles* a mimetic influence was brought to bear upon the extra-liturgical movement, later dramatic tendencies are readily explained. If one church permitted the presentation of *Les Vierges Sages et Les Vierges Folles,* another might permit the performance of such pseudo-liturgical rites as the *Resurrection* (contained in a late twelfth century MS of the Library of Tours [25]) and the *Passion* (found in a thirteenth century MS of the Library of Munich.[26]) In these pieces there is apparently a definite attempt at characterization: the chorals of *Les Vierges* disappear and even short speaking parts (without music) are introduced. Can there be any other interpretation of these phenomena than that they are the natural results of the corruption of the liturgy by a mimetic impulse? This contamination began slowly at a time when there was possibly no religious drama save school plays and dramatic monologues, but an abundance

[24] In regard to the music of the troubadours, Miss Barbara Smythe writes (*Grove's Dictionary of Music and Musicians,* "Troubadour") : "They wrote their poems in stanzas and each stanza of a song was sung to the same melody. . . . The metrical form of the songs is very varied, but in the majority, the stanza falls into two main divisions, and the first half—often also the second half—contains two equal subdivisions, e.g., ababccd, or ababcdcd. The musical form does not always correspond exactly with the metrical form, indeed it is rare to find a repeated musical phrase in the second half of the stanza. In many songs the melody flows on without repetition through the stanza. A repeated melodic phrase in the first half is, however, often found." My arrangement of the stanzas in the preceding footnote should be compared with the music in Coussemaker.

[25] Text in Coussemaker, *Drames liturgiques,* p. 21 ff.

[26] Text in DuMéril, *Origines latines,* p. 126 ff.

of loose secular performances in the market places and at the cross roads, as the decrees of the day testify.[27]   But with the appearance of mystery and miracle plays in the early twelfth century, not far from the dates of the plays of Hilarius, these secular dramas, performed from the first without the church, probably quickened the dramatic corruption of the rites within. How zealous many ecclesiastics were to maintain the difference between the liturgy and the mystery plays, may be seen in a notable passage in Robert of Brunne's *Handlyng Synne*. Yet this same passage shows in its language that the rites were no longer strictly liturgical. Robert speaks of *playing* the Resurrection and the Nativity:

> A clerk of the order that hath the name,
> Zyf he juste, he ys to blame. . .
> hyt ys forbade hym, in the decre
> Myracles for to make or se;
> For, myracles zyf thou bygynne,
> Hyt ys a gaderyng, a syght of synne;
>   He may yn the cherche, thurgh thys resun,
> Pley the resurreccyun—
> That ys to seye, how God ros,
> God and man yn mygt and los,—
> To make men be yn beleve gode
> That he ros with fleshe and blode;
> And he may pleye, withoutyn plyght
> howe God was bore yn Yole nyght,
> To make men to beleve stedfastly
> That he lyght yn the vyrgyne Mary.
> Zif thou do hyt yn weyys or greuys
> A syght of synne truly hyt semys.
> (As) seynt Ysodre . . . seyth. . . .
> That make syche pleyys to any man
> As myracles and bourdys,
> Or tournamentys of grete prys.[28]

[27] Cf. DuCange, "Joculatores"; Reich, *Der Mimus; Monumentae Germanae Scriptores, etc.*
[28] *"Handlyng Synne" With William of Wadington's "Manuel des*

In offering this explanation of how the liturgy in certain churches became corrupted through the influence of the drama, I have neglected to point out that there were from time to time distinct efforts made to make the tropes more lyrical and religious. Such an effort was made by those trope writers who sought to imitate the excellent qualities of the Latin hymns. But this influence is clearly distinguishable from that exerted by the troubadours. For example, compare the stanzas which I have quoted above from the MS of *Les Vierges Sages et Les Vierges Folles* with these of Adam de St. Victor (ca. 1180):

1. Ecce dies celebris
   Lux succedit tenebris
   Morti resurrectio.

2. Laetis cedant tristia
   Cum sit maior gloria
   Quem prima confusio.

Adam's verses are graceful and controlled. There is no attempt at alliteration or play upon words. In all his poetry there is nothing which is not lyrical in its intention. He makes no use of dialogue and but spare use of incident. Nothing dramatic came from his school.[29] If movements of this sort shed any light on our problem, they illumine the lyrical and religious character of the true trope, and render dubious the conclusion that in it is the seed of the drama.

The preceding arguments may be briefly summarized at this point. We have seen that in origin and normal growth the extra-liturgical development was not primarily dramatic. It provided rites wherein the religious emotions

---

Pechiez" ed. by F. J. Furnival (E.E.T.S., Orig. Ser. 119, 123. Pts. 1, 2; 1909), p. 154.

[29] For a discussion of Adam de St. Victor and the influence of the Latin hymn upon the liturgy, see Wagner, *Handbook of Plainsong,* p. 236.

of the celebrant and his priestly train had opportunity for lyrical expression. But these same rites ignored the congregation as completely as if it were an assembly of dumb beasts: the people were to partake by being present, not necessarily by understanding. The language of the ritual was one which the layman could not understand. There is nothing to show that the performance of the rite was such that he could easily follow it. Because Magnin made no study of the origin or character of the true tropes, he was able to assert that they were dramas. In this, first of all, I cannot agree with him.

In the second place, we have seen that the clergy lost interest in the purity of these extra-liturgical rites during the twelfth century; this had two results: (1) the actual composition was entrusted to unskilled persons, who not infrequently preferred innovations to traditional elements; (2) these authors, lacking a zealous clergy, turned to the congregation. The new tropes had the semblance of religious rites, but were in reality semi-dramatic undertakings. Concerning these pieces I make a new issue: I believe that they represent a corruption of the liturgy by the mimetic practices of the minstrels, by the drama. I believe that, as additions to the otherwise conventional service, these pieces, which still kept a large proportion of their Latin, were bound to be unsuccessful plays. It would appear that wherever they enjoyed a long popularity the excellence of the music was responsible. I cannot agree, then, with Magnin, and especially with his followers, that wherever dramatic elements appear in the liturgy they are proof of a growth or evolution toward the mystery plays. I hold that the simpler theory of contamination is generally adequate to explain such phenomena. It would appear that the developed religious drama cannot have evolved from the liturgy.

CHAPTER IV

EASTER TROPE AND RESURRECTION PLAY COMPARED

WE HAVE followed a comprehensive argument to show that there is no dramatic growth in the liturgy which would in the course of time produce mystery plays. It is possible by an altogether different type of reasoning to reach a similar conclusion. That is, a play may be selected for direct comparison with the trope from which it is alleged to have originated and the improbability of such a development demonstrated. Let us take for this test the scene in the Chester Cycle in which the three Marys visit the tomb of Christ to embalm the body:

> *Maria Salome:*
> Alas! now marred is all my might;
> My lord, throw whom my hart was light,
> Shamfully slayne here in my sight;
> My sorrow is aye unsought.
>
> Sith I may have no other right
> Of these Devils my lord so dight
> To Balms his body that is so bright
> Boyst here have I brought.
>
> *Maria Magdalena:*
> Suster, which of us echone
> shall remove this great Stone
> that lyeth my sweet Lord uppon?
> for move it I ne may.
>
> *Maria Jacobi:*
> Sister, maystrye is it none,
> it semes to me as he were gone,

for on the Sepulcre sitteth one,
and the Stonne away.

Maria Salome:
Two children ther I see sittinge,
All of whyte is ther clothinge,
and the Stonne besyde lyinge;
Goe we neare and see!

(*Tunc ibunt et in Sepulcrum circumspicient.*)

Angelus primus:
What seeke ye, women, what seeke ye here
With weping and unlyking cheare?
Jesus, that to you was deare,
is Risen, leeve you me!

Angelus Secundus:
Be not afrayd of us in feere!
for he is gone, withoutten were
As he can you leere,
forth into Galely.

Angelus primus:
This is *the* place, be ye apayd,
That Iesu our lord was in layd;
but he is risen as he sayd,
and heathen gone away.

Angelus Secundus:
Hye you, for ought that may befall
And tell his Disciples all,
and Peter also tell you shall,
ther fynd him that you may.

Maria Magdalena:
A! hye we fast for any thinge,
and tell Peter this Tydinge;
a Blessedfull word we may bringe,
sooth if that it were.[1]

This scene, according to those who hold the liturgical theory, is derived directly from the "liturgical drama" of

[1] *The Chester Plays,* Pt. II., ed. by Matthews (E.E.T.S., Ex. Ser. 115, 1916 for 1914), p. **343** ff.

the church.[2] But of this "liturgical drama" in England,
there is only one surviving specimen, the Winchester
Sepulchrum, dating earlier than the religious cycles, which
for the sake of comparison, I reproduce here:

SEPULCHRUM

Dum tertia rectatur lectio, quatuor fratres induant se, quorum
unus alba indutus ac si ad aliud agendum ingrediatur, atque latan-
ter sepulchri locum adeat, ibique manu tenens palam, quietus
sedeat. Dumque tertiam percelebratur responsorium, residui
tres succedant, omnes quidem cappis induti, turribula cum incensu
manibus gestantes ac pedetemptim ad similtudinem querentium
quid, veniant ante locum sepulchri. Aguntur enim haec ad imi-
tationem angeli sedentis in monumento atque mulierum cum
aromatibus venientum ut ungerent corpus Ihesu. Cum ergo ille
residens tres velut erraneos ac aliquid querentes viderit sibi
adproximare, incipiat mediocri voce dulcisono cantare:

> *Quem queritis?*

Quo decantato fine tenus, respondeat hi tres uno ore:

> *Ihesum Nazarenum.*

Quibus ille:

> *Non est hic; surrexit, sicut praedixerat:*
> *Ite, nuntiate quia surrexit a mortuis.*

Cuius iussionis voce vertant se ille tres ad chorum dicentes:

> *Alleluia! resurrexit Dominus.*

Dicto hoc, rursus ille residens, velut revocans illos dicat antiphonam:

> *Venite, et videte locum.*

Haec vero dicens surgat, et erigat velum, ostendatque eis locum
cruce nudatum, sed tantum linteamina posita quibus crux involuta
erat. Quo viso, deponant turribula quae gestauerant in eodem
sepulchro, sumantque linteum et extendant contra clerum, ac

---

[2] By "derived" I mean that the play has either been developed by
the elaborations of definite playwrights or has grown by natural
accumulation in presentation. Both theories are untenable.

veluti ostendentes quod surrexit Dominus et iam non sit illo involutus, hanc canant antiphonam:

Surrexit Dominus de sepulchro.

Superpoantque linteum altari. Finita antiphona, Prior conguadens pro triumpho Regis nostri, quod, devicto morte, surrexit, incipiat hymnum:

Te, Deum, laudamus.

Quo incepto, una pulsantur omnia signa.[3]

The ultimate sources of the Chester Resurrection scene and of this Winchester *Sepulchrum* are, of course, the Gospels. By comparing the rite and the play in turn with Matthew 28:1, 8; Mark 16:1, 8; Luke 23:55, 56; 24:1, 12; and John 20:1, 18, we shall see that each author has made an altogether independent use of the texts.

A. THE SEPULCHRUM

The quiet entrance of the brother who is to play the angel of God is probably taken from Mark 16:5, rather than from Matthew 28:2, 3. So, too, is the attire of the angel; that of the brethren representing the Marys seems traditional. The palm is an important bit of extraneous symbolism, found neither in the Gospel accounts nor in the mystery plays. The three Marys bearing incense may be from Mark 16:1. But for the question *Quem queritis?* the troper does not seem to have gone to the Gospels at all. In Mark and Matthew the question is not asked, while the query QUID *quaeritis?* of Luke 24:5 obviously does not appear to be the source. In John 20:15, Jesus asks Mary Magdalene, *"quid ploras? quem* QUAERIS?*"* but it seems scarcely credible that the liturgist would do the Gospel the violence *consciously* of giving the speech of Jesus to

[3] Text, J. Q. Adams, *op. cit.*, pp. 9, 10. It is taken "from the *Regularis Concordia* of St. Ethelwold, written between 965 and 975." But see my suggestion as to the date of this piece, page 28 above.

the Angel. Rather, I should say, we have here conclusive proof that the liturgist worked not from the Gospels directly, but only through a careless recollection of them. Was the musician-author more interested in the musical composition, perhaps, than in the words? Professor Adams expands the question and its answer by the customary epithets, *Christicolae* and *caelicolae*. But neither epithet is in any of the Gospels. I cannot agree, therefore, with Chambers (II, 9) that the *Quem quaeritis* trope "is based closely upon the Gospels." To return to the *Sepulchrum:* The dulcet voice is that of Mark's young man, of course, rather than from the fearful angel of Matthew. *"Non est hic, etc."*, sung by the angel, is from Matthew 28:5, 6, but the song of the Marys is not in any of the Gospels. It certainly is not suggested by Matthew 28:8, the most likely passage, for the Marys are there reported as going *cum timore*. The fear element is wholly obliterated; the remainder of the *Sepulchrum* is a pæan of rejoicing. The *Venite, et videte locum* is from Matthew 28:6. The "stage business" following the anthem grows naturally out of it, but is symbolical rather than dramatic. The *Te Deum laudamus* and the chiming of the bells are a natural climax to the emotional direction of the *Sepulchrum*.

This analysis of the *Sepulchrum* indicates that the composer (I use 'composer' advisedly, for this is a song service) wrote only from a recollection of the Scriptures, and that if he consulted them at all, he drew his most important material from the Gospel of St. Mark. This is significant, for this gospel best supplies material of a tone suited to the ultimate purpose, the triumphant rejoicing, the *jubilation*, of the *Sepulchrum*. If bits were taken from Matthew, only such items were selected as would be in keeping with the emotional trend of the service. The element of fear which predominates in Matthew does not appear in the rite. No use whatever appears to be made of the Gospels of Luke and John.

B. Chester Resurrection

A study of the Chester Resurrection will reveal, I believe, that the dramatist had no thought of the *Quem quaeritis* when he wrote this scene but was solely occupied with making a harmony for the layman out of the varying Gospel versions. It should be noted that all the Gospels are employed and in such a manner as to give probability to the conclusion that the dramatist had them before him as he worked. His method, then, is the direct converse of that of the composer of the *Sepulchrum*.

As before, the three Marys are taken from Mark 16:1. The lament of Maria Salome (and that of the other Marys, which I have not included in my excerpt) is probably suggested by the weeping Magdalene in John 20:11, 18. The balm for Christ's body is in all the Gospels. That the stone was before the door when the Marys approached the tomb is indicated by the sequence of events in Matthew 28:1, 2 (also compare Mary Magdalene's query in the play with Mark 16:3: *Quis revolvet nobis ab ostio monumenti?*); but that it was Mary Magdalene who began the conversation in regard to the great stone before the sepulchre the dramatist finds indicated by placing Mark 16:4 beside John 20:1.

Following this, we have a curious passage admirably illustrating the dramatist's effort to harmonize his source material. It will be remembered that in Matthew 28:2, "the Angel of the Lord descended from heaven, and came and rolled back the stone from the door, and sat upon it" (*Angelus enim Domini descendit de coelo: at acceddens*

revolvit lapidem, et sedebat super eum); that in Mark
16:5 the Marys "saw a young man sitting on the right
side, clothed in a long white garment; and they were af-
frighted" (*in monumentem viderunt juvenem sedentem in
dextris, coopertum stola candida, et obstupuerunt*); but
that in Luke 24:4, the Marys, having entered the tomb
and found the Christ gone, were much perplexed when
"*two* men stood by them in shining garments" (*ecce duo
viri steterunt secus illas illas in vestri fulgenti*); and that
finally, in John 20:12, Mary Magdalene "seeth *two* angels
in white sitting" (*Et vidit duos Angelos in albis, sedentes*).
The dramatist avoids the theological question of one or
two angels very neatly:

Maria Jacobi:	it seems to me as he were gone
	for on the Sepulchre sitteth *one* . . .
Maria Salome:	*Two* chidren ther I see sittinge
	All of whyte is ther clothinge
	And the Stonne beside lyinge;
	Goe we neare and see!

The first speech of *Angelus primus* is most important,
for it may be held to incorporate the inquiry *Quem
quaeritis?*

> *What* seeke ye, women, what seeke ye here
> with weeping and with unlyking cheare?

But see John 20:13:

> *Dicunt ei illi: Mulier, quid ploras?*

And Luke 24:5:

> *Cum timerent autem, et declinaret vultum in terram, dixerunt ad
> illas: Quid quaeritis viventem cum mortuis?*

Plainly the Chester dramatist has not the *Quem quaeritis*
in mind but is adapting the Gospels to make a single, logical account of the Sepulchre scene. In John only, does

the Christ actually appear. The dramatist ignores this
single reference and abides by the other three accounts.
The actual query of the angel is a possible reading for
Quid quaeritis? Quem quaeritis, as I have pointed out, is
not found in any of the Gospels.

"Jesus is risen!" is announced in all save John. "Be not
afrayd of us in feere!"˙ or its equivalent, is in Matthew
and Mark, but not in the Winchester *Sepulchrum.* The
reminder of *Angelus Secundus* that Jesus has gone

> *as he before you can leere*
> forth into galely

is especially reminiscent of Luke 24:6. (Luke is not used in
the *Sepulchrum.*) When *Angelus primus* shows the place
in which "Iesu our lord was . . . layd," he is not necessarily repeating a part of the *Sepulchrum;* the incident is
found in three of the Gospels. The command of the Second Angel for the Marys to tell the Disciples, especially
Peter, is in Mark 16:7. And finally, when Mary Magdalene (who occupies the most important part in the Cycle
as she does in the Holy Scriptures) says that they shall
carry "the blessedfull word . . . *sooth is that it were,*"
must we not feel that the dramatist had Luke 24:11 under
his eyes? *Et visa sunt ante illos, sicut deliramentum
verba ista: et non crediderunt illis.* Mary's doubt is a good
piece of characterization and preparation.

What, then, are our conclusions about the Chester Resurrection? Are they not (1) that the material comes directly from the four Gospels rather than from an
expansion of the *Quem quaeritis* or the Winchester
Sepulchrum; and (2) that this material was selected with
a view to giving a consistent account of the varying Gospel matter? Whenever we can discern a controlling artist

at work, as we do here, the notion of a slow evolution over a period of years must necessarily be abandoned. But more on this point later.

Wherein does the proof that a single play is not derived from a particular rite affect the whole liturgical theory? In this, as I understand it: *the liturgical theory admits no exceptions.* Natural growth is the explanation for all phenomena, and evidences of this growth should be discoverable in every mystery play. Now the Winchester *Sepulchrum* not only is the sole surviving example of the *Quem quaeritis* prior to the drama in England, but it is also a fair representative of any or all of the Easter tropes,[4] tropes from which the play, as it is asserted, could have been derived. The Chester Resurrection is generally conceded to be the earliest of the English plays on the subject, being written in the stanza characteristic of the earliest plays. Here, if anywhere, points of contact between the liturgy and the drama should be found. But here, as apparently everywhere, close examination proves these to be lacking. Because, after a most diligent search, I have found no atrophied or semi-atrophied tropes (no lines which may not as well have come from some other source) in any of the genuine plays, I again conclude that it remains to be shown precisely how the mysteries could have developed from the liturgy.

[4] All the Easter tropes are held to be derived from the St. Gall *Quem quaeritis,* in that they duplicate the language and tone of that trope. Cf. Carl Lange, *Lateinische Osterfeiern,* Munich, Stahl, 1887, 171 pp.

CHAPTER V

MARIUS SEPET AND THE EVOLUTIONISTS

IN THE early nineteenth century there were few per-
fectionists. Hence, although a number of scholars published texts illustrating the theory of Magnin, there was
no effort made then to extend or enlarge his theory. But
about the middle of the century the promulgation of the
doctrine of evolution resulted in the revival of perfectiv-
ism. While one man saw in scarpéd cliff and quarried
stone the eternal strife of God and Nature, another beheld
in everything—art, religion, and science—a sure progress
toward better things. Literary criticism, of course, did not
escape this influence. But critics who took over the
"growth" theory for the various types of literature failed
to appreciate that the doctrine was only imperfectly ap-
plicable to literary craftsmanship, where individuality and
revolt are ever to be reckoned with.

Marius Sepet, the most important figure after Magnin
in the history of the liturgical theory, came under the influence of these scientific ideas. This is apparent in the
opening lines of *Les Prophètes du Christ*,[1] the first edition
of which appeared in 1867:

The brilliant and ingenious critique of M. Charles Magnin
has clearly demonstrated the bonds, vaguely seen before him,
which attach the medieval drama to the Catholic liturgy. The

[1] *Bibliothèque de l'École de Chartes, XXVIII.* I use throughout this chapter a reprint, *Les Prophètes du Christ, étude sur les
origines du théâtre au moyen âge,* Paris, Didier, 1878, 139 pp.

60

publication of the oldest texts by MM. Jubinal, DuMéril, Monmerquè and Michel, Coussemaker, and Luzarche, have only confirmed the opinions of Magnin and the results which he brought to light. Is it possible to prove . . . that by a series of logical developments, the offices tranform themselves into dramas less and less liturgical, until the day comes when mystery and liturgy are not synonymous terms: in a word, that the theatre of the Middle Ages issued from the religion of the Middle Ages, in the same fashion and following the same laws as did the ancient theatre in issuing from the ancient religion? [2]

And again:

We shall have the pleasure of demonstrating *scientifically* that the *Prophètes du Christ* of the eleventh century are nothing more than the first edition of the mystery of the *Vieux Testament;* . . . that from its birth in the Church to its fall in the Renaissance, the medieval drama did not cease to elaborate the same ideas, under the influence of three laws which dominated it:
(1) The law of assimilation and amplification;
(2) The law of disaggregation;
(3) The law of agglutination or of juxtaposition;
laws, which, acting in a sense contrary to each other, but equalizing themselves from time to time, have produced that prodigious variety of medieval dramatic texts to which only science can and must restore unity.[3]

Prior to the influence of science upon literary criticism, the statement of Magnin, that the drama grew from the Latin "mysteries" of the church, was quite satisfactory. But it was now found to have surprising deficiencies. For example, in the mystery plays were scenes which were without germ or parallel in the liturgy. Satan's unsuccessful revolution, the tempting of Adam and Eve, the slaying of Abel, Abraham's offering, Noah's difficulties with his wife, etc.—*none* of the many Old Testament epi-

[2] Note again the argument from the analogy of the Greek theater.
[3] Sepet, *op. cit.,* p. 27. The italics are Sepet's own.

sodes which were part and parcel of the mysteries—had been traced to the liturgy. Notable scenes present in the mystery plays which dealt with Christ, moreover, were lacking in the liturgical accounts of His life. But inasmuch as the Christmas tropes heralded the birth of Christ and those of Easter his resurrection, the gaps in pseudo-Gospel history as told by the tropes gave the critics far less concern than the great lack of tropes based on stories from the Old Testament. How could the slaying of Abel have originated in the Christmas or Easter liturgy, the primary germ plasm of everything dramatic? It required great ingenuity to establish the necessary connections. Yet the thing was done in brilliant fashion.

In 1867, Sepet produced an explanation which was outwardly so satisfactory that it has not been examined critically from that day to this. He discovered a *lectio* in which various Old Testament characters appeared as prophets of Christ, whereupon he announced that the Old Testament plays were really appended to those originating in the Christmas liturgy as prophetic of the Saviour's coming. To substantiate his theory he produced several tropes and pseudo-tropes in which various Old Testament characters (not always the same ones) assumed rôles foretelling the birth of Christ. Each item in his proof was carefully assigned its proper relationship and the whole argument was delivered with telling force. Sepet's name is not often on our tongues today when we speak of the medieval drama; yet he is by far the most important original figure in the field. There is not an investigator from his time to ours who is not heavily indebted to him, if not for substance, at least for method and approach.

Among those who have followed Sepet are three great names: Louis Petit de Julleville, the historian of the

French theater, chiefly interested in the fifteenth century drama and not in its origins,[4] famous for his aesthetic criticism and his study of comedy;[5] Wilhelm Creizenach, German encyclopedist, whose survey of the drama is still the best;[6] and finally, Sir Edmund K. Chambers, who, working under the influence of Sir James Frazer and the *Golden Bough*, has given us what we may consider the definitive account of the folk drama, and has proved the value of a suggestion made long ago by Magnin, that the minstrel was descended from the mimus.[7] These three have accepted the results of Magnin and Sepet in good faith and have built their own work more or less upon them.

Then there have been the extremists, evolutionists *par excellence;* these latter are too numerous to call by roll, hence we shall have to be satisfied with example. Mr. Alfred W. Pollard not only believes that the mysteries may be traced to the liturgy, but also holds that "each cycle as it has come down to us must be regarded rather as an *organic growth* than as the work of a single author."[8] Dr. Paul E. Kretzmann—sturdy son of German parents, who in the course of the Great War saw fit to accuse Chambers of theft from *Creizenach!*—discovers liturgical dithyrambs "in all those parts of the medieval drama which others have neglected."[9] Finally, Professor G. R.

[4] *Les Mystères; histoire du théâtre en France au moyen âge,* Paris, Hachette, 1880, 2 vols.

[5] *Les Comédiens en France au moyen âge,* Paris, Cerf, 1885.

[6] *Geschichte des Neueren Dramas,* Halle, Niemeyer, 1893, 5 vols., Vol. I.

[7] *The Medieval Stage,* Oxford, Clarendon Press, 1903, 2 vols.

[8] *English Miracle Plays,* Oxford, Clarendon Press, 1890, p. xxx.

[9] *The Liturgical Element in the Earliest Forms of the Medieval Drama* (Univ. of Minn. Studies in Lang. and Lit., No. 4), Minneapolis, 1916, 170 pp.

Coffman, implicitly accepting the growth theory for the mysteries, seeks and finds (so he thinks) a liturgy from which the miracle plays likewise grew.[10]

This goes to show how thoroughly Marius Sepet's work has established itself in half a century. There have been quarrels a plenty over minor points advanced by later investigators; but nowhere in the great mass of literature which has been written have I come upon a single statement fundamentally damaging to Sepet—quarrels, I say, but no criticism.

Sepet's case could with justice be disposed of very summarily on three counts: (1) it presupposes that the theories of Magnin are correct as to the relationships existing between the tropes and the drama; (2) it makes no attempt to synchronize its statements with the facts of liturgical history, such as we have studied;[11] and (3) it assumes the existence of material essential for its ends.[12] On the other hand, it is the keystone of the arch of modern criticism in regard to the medieval drama—the model of the modern method. It deserves better than swift dismissal, for the critical theory may be quite correct even though the author has based his whole argument upon the dubious reasoning of Magnin. That is, the principle of unpremeditated growth may actually be the most important factor in the development of the drama, as of any form of literature. It is a question of esthetics as well as of source-study. Moreover, Sepet's theory is unique in that it starts with a *lectio*, or lesson, rather than with a trope

[10] *A New Theory Concerning the Origin of the Miracle Play*, Menasha, Wis., 1914.

[11] Failure to date accurately his specimens shows Sepet careless, if not ignorant, of liturgical history.

[12] See his discussion of the law of juxtaposition, *op. cit.* pp. 84–86.

as the germ of later developments. For these reasons, and for others which will appear in season, I propose to analyze Sepet's *Les Prophètes du Christ* rather thoroughly here.

Aside from his intention to prove scientifically [13] that the theater of the Middle Ages issued from the religion of the Middle Ages, just as the theater of antiquity issued from the religion of antiquity, Sepet declared as his purpose, "more especially to show how a sermon, having for its subject the Nativity of Christ, which formed, in a great number of dioceses in the Middle Ages, one of the lessons for Christmas, transforms itself into a liturgical mystery, into a semi-liturgical mystery inside and outside the church, and finally appears almost unchanged in a great dramatic cycle of the fifteenth century." [14]

The "sermon" is a apocryphal *lectio* attributed to St. Augustine which Sepet discovered in a manuscript breviary of the diocese of Arles,[15] bearing in red ink the title *Sermo beati Augustini episcopi de Natale Domini, lectio sexta*. The only evidence which Sepet was able to adduce as to its date was the character of the writing, which seemed to him to be of the twelfth century.[16] In the *lectio*, the Jews and the Pagans (even Golias) are furnished with proof that Christ is the Messiah, which they had doubted. One by one, twelve prophets are summoned to declare Christ the promised Lord: *Isaiah, Jeremiah, Daniel, Moses, David Habakkuk, Simeon, Zachariah* and *Elisabeth, John the Baptist, Virgil,* and *the Sibyl*—a fantastic group.

It is essential, [says Sepet] to call attention to the fact that

---

[13] *Op. cit.,* pp. 2, 27, etc.

[14] *Op. cit.,* p. 2. Note that Sepet uses the word "mystery" to describe all rites which he wishes to prove dramatic.

[15] Bibliothèque Nationale, Fonds Latin, 1018.

[16] *Les Prophètes,* p. 3. Sepet prints a text of the sermon.

the sermon is here a lesson, and that the office is that of Christmas. . . . Thus it is not with a sermon *preached* that we have to do, but with a sermon *read*, or better recited, intoned or varied, analogous to those which we are still able to hear any Sunday in our churches when the Epistle or the Gospel is read at the High Mass.

This intonation, or varied intonation, which is not without kin, distant to be sure, in the measured declamation *(mélopée)* used in the tragedy of Antiquity, completely changes the character of the piece. It transforms the *lectio* beyond all question into a monologue; but it is in fact a monologue declaimed by a special actor who has charge of all the rôles. It changes the sermon into a *recitatif.*[17]

We should think the analogy of the Greek method a rather curious way of proving this lesson a dramatic recitation if the investigator had not produced further evidence. And this he does produce. Two of the prophecies —those of Isaiah and Jeremiah—are marked by red capitals in the margin of the manuscript, an indication to the reader, so Sepet thinks, to vary his voice to suit the personage. But does this exhaust the reasons that could be given for red characters in the margin? And why should only the first two prophecies be accorded this treatment? One must regard the evidence that this piece was a dramatic recitation as rather slender. Yet Chambers, without adding one iota more of proof, decides that "the dramatic form of this *lectio* possibly led to its being chanted instead of read, and distributed to several voices in the manner of the Passions from Palm Sunday to Good Friday."[18]

[17] *Op. cit.,* p. 9.

[18] *Med. Stage,* Vol. II, p. 53. The *lectio* was probably *intoned,* not that it should be dramatic, but that it should be *heard* in all parts of the church. "I do not include under the term liturgical chant," writes Mgr. L. Duchesne, "the recitative or intoning of the lections or such of the prayers as are said aloud. This practice may

Nothing is more apparent than that Chambers relied implicitly upon Sepet for the text of the lesson and for all his information concerning the manuscript. He obviously had never seen the Breviary of Arles.[19] *Certain facts, important facts in regard to that Breviary, Sepet failed to report,* and his failure has led many a scholar astray. May I call attention to some of these facts which my own examination of the manuscript has elicited—facts which have an important bearing upon our discussion?

The first third of the book (folios 6-111) is taken up by "hymns," or two-part chants, of which one part is always indicated by a red letter and the other by a blue. The latter portion, the bulk of the book, is assigned exclusively to *lectiones,* our "sermon" being merely one of hundreds. Yet occasionally at the end of the *lectiones* appear lines of music accompanied by words. There is but one possible way of interpreting the performance of this music,—after the lesson was read, the song must have been supplied as a response. This was the invariable practice from the earliest times in regard to the recitation of the *lectiones.*[20] The MS itself bears out this interpretation, for there is no use of blue ink to indicate antiphonal singing, as was the case with the two-part chants. Red ink capitals and the music thus serve to distinguish the simple responses

be very ancient. It was necessarily introduced as soon as the Christian assemblies became very large, and thus rendered it difficult for the officiating minister or reader to make himself heard." (*Christian Worship: A study of the Latin Liturgy up to the Time of Charlemagne,* trans. by M. L. McClure, London, Society for Promoting Christian Knowledge, 1919 [593 pp.], p. 117.) There is a striking difference between this monotonous intoning and the "mélopée" and "chanting" supposed by Sepet and Chambers.

[19] Biblio. Nat. MS Lat. 1018.

[20] For example, Migne, *Patrol. Lat.* Vol. CLXXIX, col. 737.

from the lesson proper, which, being without music, must have been read or intoned. There is no evidence for declamation.

Sepet has failed to mention a fact which materially affects Chambers' theory that the different prophecies were assigned various choristers. The prophecy of *Sibilla* is accompanied by music! Being all incorporated in the body of the lesson, none of the other prophecies have this musical notation, and the plain inference is that this was the only one that was sung, the only one possibly not assigned to the reader of the lessons. It, in all probability, was given to the choir as a response. The pseudo-Augustinian "sermon" is like the other lessons in the breviary, in that there is no division of the material save for the song at the end. Consequently I doubt Chambers' theory and I see no reason for supposing that the piece was presented with a variation of intonation, as Sepet thinks.

Furthermore, the conventional placing of this particular *lectio* in the midst of the other lessons for the day offers no justification for the supposition that it alone was performed in a special manner. In other words, since it was customary to recite five or seven lessons with their responses *in Vigilis Natalis Domini,* and since this was customarily the fourth or sixth lesson, this *lectio* might easily have been given in a perfunctory manner or with the indifference and haste which sometimes characterize the readings of the lessons today. If it was thus buried in the ritual for the day, and so recited, the *lectio* can hardly be described as dramatic.[21]

---

[21] Cf. Migne, *loc. cit.;* Mabillon, Vol. II, p. 118. "In Vigilia Natalis Domini ad matutinum inviatorium, Christus adveniet nobis, venite adoremus. Ant. *Dominus dixit ad me;* psalmus, *Quare fremuerunt gentes.* Ant. *In sole posuit tabernaculum;* psalmus,

The manuscript of this Arles Breviary appears, upon examination, to have been prepared in the customary manner: first the bulk of the text was carefully completed in dark ink, purple pencilings being left to aid in supplying the rubrics, page ornamentations, and so on. These were afterwards [22] inserted somewhat hastily [23] in colored inks. The notations which stand for Isaiah and Jeremiah were put in at this later time. *But Sepet neglects to say that there are no purple pencilings for them—the only omission of this kind which I was able to discover in the volume.* That is, the marginal notations are apparently the unpremeditated work of a scribe. Ought Sepet, then, to infer as much as he does from them? Certainly it cannot be claimed from them that the author of the *lectio* had any intention that the piece should be dialogued.

It does not seem at all probable that the abbreviations for Isaiah and Jeremiah are indications for voice change,

Coeli enarrant. Ant. *Elevamini portae aeternales;* psalmus, *Domini est terra.* Versus, *Hodie scientis quia reniet Dominus* et quinque lectiones et quinque responsoria. Quarta lectio, sermo S. Augustini, *Vos, inquam, convenio, o Judaei.* In quarta cantantur sibyllini versus, *Judicii signum, tellus sudore madescit.* Quinta de homilia, etc."

The method of reciting this lesson must have been perfectly plain to Sepet, for he refers the reader to Edmundi Marténe, *De Antiquis Ecclesiae Ritibus* ([Antwerp, 1737, 4 vols.] Tome III, cap. XII), who, in citing some unusual uses of the Sibylline verses, says, "etiam ex ordinario Narbonesi debent cantari circa finem nonnae lectiones a melioribus vocibus clericorum & ipsis cantatis resumi lectio ab eo qui primo illam inceperat." Cf. *Les Prophètes du Christ,* p. 2.

[22] Though the purple pencilings go nearly to the end of the volume, the scribe who inked them completed only two-thirds (roughly) of his work.

[23] The red ink is carelessly placed at times (folio 131 verso); at other times the folios are left untouched (127 verso, 128 recto).

as Sepet supposes. They are in the margin, opposite the prophecies of Isaiah and Jeremiah, which, though first in the "sermon," come at the bottom of the page. It looks as if the scribe with the red ink, a careless fellow, had noted them as authorities taken for the text of the "sermon," [24] then turning the page, saw his mistake and made no further notations. This is an obvious inference from the manuscript. But there is a more conclusive way of showing that the scribe was citing what he supposed were authorities. The *lectio*, as I have pointed out, is derived ultimately from a long sermon, *Contra Judaeos, Paganos et Arianos: Sermo de Symbolo*, of which it is the eleventh chapter. This chapter is entitled, *Contra Judaeos, ex Isaia et Jeremia.*[25] Surely this title is the source of the marginal notations which are so important to Sepet's case. It would thus appear that Sepet had offered no substantial evidence to show that the *lectio* was either dialogued or declaimed in a manner to suggest dialogue.

This *lectio*, says Sepet, "is the basis for all my work." [26] By this statement he means that he takes it for the source of all the tropes and the mystery plays which deal with the prophets. But earlier than this *lectio* is the long sermon, or better *tract*, likewise attributed to St. Augustine, known as the *Sermo Contra Judaeos, Paganos, et Arianos.*[27] Containing the most familiar arguments against the heretics, it is a defense of the Catholic belief in the Trinity. This tract, never used in any liturgical fashion, does, however, contain every word of the Arles *lectio*, being, of course, the

[24] Many of the *lectiones* in the Arles Breviary have the Gospel texts, etc., in the red ink titles.

[25] Migne, *Patrol. Lat.* Vol. XLII, col. 1116 ff.

[26] *Les Prophètes*, p. 3.

[27] Printed in Migne, *op. cit.*, Vol. XLII, col. 1116 ff.

accepted source of that piece.[28] Sepet has not advanced
any reason why we should accept the *lectio* in preference to
the tract as the ultimate source of all the pieces which he
believes based upon it. He knew very well that because
of the identity of language in tract and *lectio* it would be
almost impossible for any one to take issue with him
on this score. But should we not naturally be inclined to
favor the tract as a source, because of its early accessi-
bility and popularity? I leave the question for the reader
to decide. One thing is certain, the question is too important for Sepet to have ignored altogether.

The *lectio* presented, Sepet produces as its first offspring
a trope of the *Prophets of Christ*, according to the usage of
the monastery of St. Martial of Limoges. At the head of
the piece appear the rimed Latin verses:

> Omnes gentes
> Congaudentes
> Dent cantum leticie!
> Deus homo fit
> De domo Davit
> Natus hodie.

This trope is then, in the first place, "a dialogued song,
destined to celebrate the birth of Christ 'natus hodie'; it is
also a trope of the office of Christmas."

"I affirm, in the second place," he continues, "that the
general drift of the trope is the same as that of the
sermon:"

Determined to be obstinate in their bad faith, the Jews who
refuse to recognize Jesus Christ for the Messiah, have recalled
to them in dramatic form, all the testimony that the prophets
of their Law have rendered concerning the Saviour; after which
are evoked the Gentiles who likewise predict his coming, with
the purpose of overwhelming the Jews by the greatest number

[28] Admitted by Sepet, *op. cit.*, p. **3**.

of proofs, and of convincing the pagan nations themselves. . . .
Such is the subject and purpose of the sermon.

Now what is the subject of the trope? The following verses
give it to us:

"O Judei
Verbum Dei
Vestri legis
Testi regis
Audite per ordinem.

Et vos, gentes
Non credentes
Peperisse virginem
Vestre gentis
Documentis
Pellite caliginem."

The identity of the subject is evident and I do not need further to demonstrate it.[29]

In the third place, I say that the personages are the same.

What are the personages of the sermon?

I put aside for the moment those whom I call the *disputants*,
that is to say, Augustine and the Jews. We shall find them in
other tropes. The *objective* characters of the sermon, that is
to say, the essential actors of the drama, are the prophets. Augustine is only the evoker; and in our trope, the choragus—
lector or *precentor*—replaces him. But the prophets successively evoked, in the sermon are: *Isaiah, Jeremiah, Daniel,
Moses, David, Habakkuk, Simeon, Zachariah and Elisabeth, John
the Baptist, Virgil, Nebuchadnezzar*, and the *Sibyl*.

Those of the trope are: *Israel, Moses, Isaiah, Jeremiah,
Daniel, Habakkuk, David, Simeon, Elisabeth, John the Baptist
Virgil, Nebuchadnezzar, Sibyl*.

A character has been added to the trope: *Israel*. But is not
he evoked, or at least mentioned, in the sermon: ". . . debit eam
Jacob puero suo et Israel dilecto suo . . ."?

A person has been withdrawn: *Zachariah*. But is not one
able to say that he is still present in the person of his spouse,
Elisabeth, and besides, we shall find him present in other versions of the *Prophets of Christ*.

[29] *Op. cit.*, pp. 15, 16.

As for the order followed in the summoning, it is not exactly the same, but that should not astonish us. Evidently the anonymous poet, without doubt a master or scholar of the monastic school of St. Martial of Limoges, who turned into rime the sermon attributed to St. Augustine, followed with some latitude his source material. . . .[30]

I affirm, in the fourth place, that the rôles, that is to say the speeches placed in the mouths of the prophets, are, with only one exception, very nearly the same in the trope and in the sermon, and that exception explains itself very easily. I omit *Israel,* who figures only incidentally in the sermon, being merely named in the prophecy of *Jeremiah.* The exception of which I spoke is the prophecy of *Isaiah.* In the sermon:

"Ecce, inquit virgo in utero concipiet et pariet filium et vocabitur nomen ejus Hemanuhel." (Isaiah 8:4.)

In the trope:

> "Est necesse
> Virga Jesse
> De radice provei;
> Flors deinde
> Surget inde
> Qui est Spiritus Dei."

This is a transformation into rimed Latin verse of the text of *Isaiah:* "Egredietur virga de radice Jesse et flos de radice ejus ascendet et requiescat super eum Spiritus Domini" (Isaiah 11:1, 2). But these words of *Isaiah* were in the usage of the liturgy of Christmas, and they sang them in all our churches, which explains very easily how they were first substituted. . . .[31]

I say, in the fifth place, that in comparing the two texts one finds a sufficient number of resemblances in the details, to give, with those resemblances already signalized, *an invincible force* to the relationship.[32]

Let us pause here for a moment to ask ourselves if Sepet has established his first step. Ignoring the exceptions to every resemblance, just what do his five similarities estab-

[30] *Ibid.,* p. 16.   [31] *Ibid.,* p. 17.   [32] *Ibid.,* p. 22.

lish? Do they prove necessarily that the trope is the first
offspring of the *lectio?* No, hardly that; every item in his
proof goes to show a relationship existing between the two
pieces, but not that the direction of indebtedness must be
from "sermon" to trope. Sepet is silent on this point, or
rather, he has assumed what he should have proved.

It is entirely possible that the trope may have been created *independently* of the *lectio* and based directly upon
the long tract attributed to St. Augustine, which, as I have
pointed out, is the source of the *lectio* itself. This would
account for every resemblance between the trope and the
lectio.

Finally, it is entirely possible that the trope may have
been created *prior* to the *lectio.* Sepet's own admission
places the date of both manuscripts in the twelfth century.
But, as we have seen from our study of the liturgy, the
monastery of St. Martial of Limoges would be more likely
to welcome innovation, and at an earlier date, than any
single *church* in the Roman diocese of Arles, where the
lectio must be placed. Not only would the Church authorities be opposed to such an innovation, but those of Arles,
because of its proximity to the favored Avignon, would be
especially opposed. Because the trope was a monastic rite,
while the *lectio* was diocesan, I believe that the trope appeared earlier.

Not only is the trope of St. Martial a rimed trope, but it
is rimed with extraordinary internal patterns, with repeti-
tions and alliterations. For example:

> Omnes *gentes*
> Congau*dentes*
> *Dent* cantum leti*cie!*
> *Deus homo fit*
> *De domo Davit*
> Natus *hodie.*

Or this:

> O Ju*dei*
> Verbum *Dei*
> V*e*stre *legis*
> T*e*ste *regis*
> Audi*te* per ordinem etc.

Opulence of this sort does not belong to the earliest rimed tropes, such as those of 1125. It belongs to a later period, I should judge, when mere rime no longer satisfied and the poets were striving for new effects. Somewhere between 1180 and 1200 will serve for the St. Martial of Limoges *Prophetae*, with the probability that the latter date is the more likely one.[33] Is it not possible that the *lectio* may be later than this? Yet there is the unsubstantiated testimony of Sepet that the manuscript is in a "twelfth century" hand. In this contention I find nothing, however, that would prevent dating the *lectio* as late as 1250. One community, Arles for instance, might be conservative as to its chirography. The scribe might have been an elderly man, or he might have habitually affected an archaic style of penmanship. At this point I do not wish to attempt dating the "sermon"; I merely desire to demonstrate how flimsy is the case which Sepet thought had *"invincible force."*

Sepet held that the drama has its birth with this St. Martial *Prophetae*. His reasons for holding this appear to be based upon an inadequate appreciation of the liturgy:

In the trope, on the other hand, dialogue is evident, *because without dialogue the trope would have no reason for being.* . . . The trope still places the names of the persons at the head of the evocation, and unites the responses to the queries by the word RESPONSUM which *alone* [italics mine] indicates the dia-

[33] "Completely rimed offices belong to the end of the twelfth and the beginning of the thirteenth centuries." Peter Wagner, *Handbook of Plainsong*, p. 270.

logue, and is only the word *inquit* transformed into a rubric.
For example:

ISRAEL

Israel, vir lenis, inque,
De Christi, quid nosti, firme.

RESPONSUM

Dux de Juda non tolletur
Donec adsit qui mittetur,
Salutare Dei verbum
Expectabunt gentes mecum.

MOSES

Legislator, hunc propinqua
Et de Christo prome digna.

RESPONSUM

Dabit Deus vobis vatem, etc.[34]

If I understand Sepet, he contends that different members
of the choir take the parts of the *Prophetae* labelled *Responsum*, thus assuming in turn the rôles of *Israel*, *Moses*,
and so on. If that is not his meaning here, at least it is
implicit in his later discussion. Nothing more clearly shows
Sepet's unfamiliarity with the liturgy. This is a simple
example of antiphonal singing. In such a piece, according
to Wagner, *Responsum* was the customary signal for the
soloist or master of the choir.[35] He took all the parts
labeled *Responsum* (those parts which Sepet believes were
assigned to different singers), while the invocations (vari-
ously labeled) were given to the full choir. If the responses
were assigned to various persons, as Sepet thinks, why are
they not designated by the individual names? Liturgical
tradition, and the study of any breviary, both favor the

[34] *Les Prophètes*, p. 23.
[35] *Handbook of Plainsong*, p. 49.

interpretation which I suggest, and he who would put another upon the *Prophetae* must assume an uncomfortable burden of proof.

His first step established to his satisfaction, Sepet announces three laws which he finds operative in the further evolution of the drama from the trope. They are:

1. The law of assimilation and amplification.
2. The law of disaggregation.
3. The law of agglutination or of juxtaposition.

He illustrates the operation of these laws in turn.

1. Development by assimilation and amplification is illustrated by the *Procession de l'Ane* of Rouen, the text of which no longer exists, but may be found reproduced in DuCange, at the word *Festum asinorum*. This procession derives its name from the ass ridden into the church by the prophet Balaam, which was in the eyes of the spectators (as it is in ours) the most novel feature of the program.[36] Ample directions are given for the separate recitation of parts, and for the thorough costuming of the characters.[37] This procession, Sepet thinks, took place at Christmas, although DuCange, who alone saw the manuscript, states definitely that it occurred on the seventh of January. We know that it was a custom of the Roman Church (a custom always frowned upon by the cardinals, but winked at locally) to allow the freedom of the sanctuary for their rites, at least one day in the year, to all those who were not in orders, but were connected with the ecclesiastical establishment: clerks with their first tonsure, boys of the outer school, grooms and servants. In these rites the clergy took no part. At first the ceremonies were conducted with gravity, but quickly all sorts of burlesque came in, leading

[36] Sepet, *op. cit.*, p. 28.
[37] *Ibid.*, p. 41 ff.

ultimately to the Feast of Fools, the Election of the Boy Bishop, etc.[38] The *Procession* of Rouen, which is of the earlier half of the thirteenth century, does not seem to contain more than a touch or two of the humorous. Here the ass is symbolical of the humble orders celebrating their holiday. One must not forget that it was no uncommon thing for painters to place the head of an ass next that of Christ in pictures of the Nativity. Sepet remarks in regard to the character of the *Procession:* "The nature of this representation, the directions for presentation, are both incontestably liturgical"—by which he must mean that a sense of solemn ritual pervades the piece.[39] Yet we must not forget that this rite in no sense belongs to the liturgy of any church.

The *Procession*, I believe, has a two-fold source: (1) The text is an ignorant imitation of the liturgy (Sepet complains that DuCange's copy is "frightful and nearly unintelligible"); and (2) the costuming and expanded scenes are imitated from the drama. But first let us see how Sepet accounts for the new features in this *Procession of the Ass* of Rouen:

(A) Assimilation. The action consists purely and simply in a defile of the prophets, who come, each in his turn, to recite their prophecies. But the number of prophets, confined to a dozen in the trope of St. Martial . . . was easily multiplied with the aid of the Holy Books and the commentaries. In order to develop the drama without discarding the form, it sufficed to introduce a number of prophets up to then neglected. . . . Thus at Rouen, although *Israel* disappears, we find added *Amos, Aaron, Balaam, Samuel, Hosea, Joel, Abdi, Jonah, Michah, Nahum, Sophonias, Agee, Zachariah, the son of Barachias, Eze-*

[38] Felix Bourquelot, *Office de la fête des fous de Sens,* Sens, 1856; Chambers, *Med. Stage,* Vol. I, (Chs. XIII, XIV, XV) p. 274 ff.
[39] *Les Prophètes,* p. 47.

kiel and *Malachi*. We find also *Zachariah*, the father of St. John the Baptist, but he had been evoked in the sermon.[40]

There is one immediate objection to accepting the law of Assimilation, and that is this: How can we deduce a law from one or two examples of this kind of expansion? Sepet desires to show the functioning of a natural law, yet all the evidence for his law is contained in the single piece in which he wishes to demonstrate that it is operative. Logicians have a hard epithet for this type of reasoning. Furthermore, why may not the addition of characters be merely for the purpose of prolonging the mock service in order that a greater number might have a share? I do not insist that this is the reason for the additional prophecies, but it is certainly a simple explanation which Sepet has ignored.

(B) Amplification. Sepet finds another force at work in the leaven. Certain rôles, such as those of Balaam and Nebuchadnezzar *"expand themselves"* because of their popularity. Thus, in the *Processional*, the rôle of Nebuchadnezzar is amplified into a little drama.[41]

To the law of amplification may be interposed the same objection that has been raised against the law of assimilation. A sufficient number of examples has not been produced by the author for the demonstration of his law. Furthermore, it seems probable that the character of Balaam was enlarged because of the significant part his rôle occupies in the ritual. As for the expanded Nebuchadnezzar rôle, the dramatic touches, etc., may not these features *equally well* be the first indications of an outside force, that of the drama, making its initial intrusion upon

[40] *Ibid.*, pp. 28, 29.
[41] *Ibid.*, p. 35 ff.

the "liturgy"? Is not this the point where we should expect the influence of the drama first to be felt—on a liturgy, which was not a liturgy at all, but a *lay ritual* performed by persons, who, as I hope to show, acted in the regular drama?

In summary, the *Procession of the Ass* is late enough to have been built upon the St. Martial of Limoges *Prophetae*. Individual genius seems to have had as much a share in its expansion as any natural force which may be proposed. The dramatic touches are open to two explanations, the influence of the true drama seeming preferable to me (nothing is demonstrable here) to Sepet's theory of internal and natural growth.

2. As Sepet remarks, his second law, that of disaggregation, implies in its very name, a counterforce to the forces of assimilation and amplification. From the scientific standpoint assumed by Sepet, however, it is quite otherwise:

Returning to the study of the dramatic movement which has transformed the legend of the *Prophets of Christ* of the sermon attributed to St. Augustine . . . into the little dramas of Balaam and Nebuchadnezzar within the larger drama, we will attempt to explain the progress that the movement ought to make, the argument being that this movement ought to act in the same way upon the other prophecies, to transform them in the same manner. The liturgist who, in this or that diocese, had charge of altering the old dramas, that is to say, of amplifying them, because they no longer satisfied the larger and larger crowd of spectators, adopted this convenient procedure: instead of limiting himself to making the prophets appear successively upon the scene to recite their prophecies, he placed many of those already there in the midst of the most striking circumstances of their lives, surrounding them by contemporary personages. . . . As a result . . . a series of little dramas grew and developed in the bosom of the action by the same procedure that the action itself grew and developed. But in proportion as these secondary scenes, as these actions within the action, grew in strength, the unity of the primitive drama was lost, until the day arrived when one of these new dramas constituted a complete action, sufficient unto itself. A rupture had to take place between it and the drama which bore it; it had to separate itself from the common body, just as a ripe fruit falls from the tree which gave it blossom. It is thus that the *Prophets of Christ* divided itself into several distinct dramas, which have nothing in common but their origin, and it is this process which I call the law of Disaggregation, which is, as one sees, a natural result of the law of Assimilation and Amplification.[42]

The operation of this law requires that the *Prophetae* not only reach the state of development manifested in the *Procession* of Rouen, but advance a step beyond the development of the Rouen ritual—that is, to use Sepet's own figure, until one of the ripened scenes falls off the tree. The Rouen *Procession of the Ass* may be dated anywhere from 1200 to 1250.[43] Drama produced from the Rouen *Processional* (or a like piece) must fall after these dates. Now Sepet presents two "dramas" that are the result of his second process: they are the *Daniel* attributed to Hilarius, and the *Daniel* found in the MS belonging to the Chapter of Beauvais. Both dramas close with a prophecy announcing the birth of Jesus, both are in Latin, both containing "paraphrases" of the prophecy of Daniel found in the *lectio*.[44]

Hilarius was a disciple of Abelard (1079–1142), as we

[42] *Ibid.,* p. 48.

[43] The MS probably belonged to the fourteenth century. Cf. Chambers, *op. cit.,* Vol. II, p. 54, note 1.

[44] Sepet, *op. cit.,* p. 51: "This prophecy is nothing else, in fact, than the paraphrase which we have cited from the text of St. Martial, copied by that of Rouen, and which is itself only a rimed version of the prophecy belonging to the sermon."

learn from his verse, which is contained in the same manuscript with his plays. The mere fact that he alludes to
his great teacher in one of his poems as if the latter were
still living does not prove that the plays are of equal antiquity; yet there is the strongest probability that they
are. Now Sepet makes no attempt to square the actual
date of the *Daniel* with the later date which his evolutionary processes (amplification, assimilation, disaggregation)
require. This would appear to be an inexplicable over-
sight.

Sepet feels that, because Daniel pronounces a prophecy
foretelling the coming of Christ, the play of Hilarius must
be connected with the pseudo-Augustinian *lectio*. But too
much must not be made of the fact that Daniel appears as
a prophet of Christ at the close of a play which surveys
the whole of the prophet's life. The Middle Ages highly
valued the powers of prophecy and divination; hence a
play dealing with a popular prophet might well be deemed
deficient if it did not close with the fullest demonstration
of these powers. In the Scriptures, moreover, Daniel is the
prophet of the Messiah (*Daniel* 9:25); and to the believing
Christian the Messiah and Christ were one. But the
prophecy which Daniel makes of the Christ is perhaps even
a paraphrase of the *lectio*, says Sepet, for it adopts two
words from the *lectio*, "*cessabit . . . unctio.*" These are
not found in the text, *Daniel* 9:24, hence they must come
from the *lectio*.[45] Now it may very well be that these two
all-important words do not appear in the Bible, but they
are found in the long pseudo-Augustinian tract, already referred to, a tract with which a pupil of Abelard certainly
might be familiar.[46] It is a curious thing that Sepet ignores

[45] *Ibid.*, p. 51.
[46] "Cum venerit," inquit, "Sanctus Sanctorum, *cessabit unctio.*"

this tract altogether when it is the most obvious source for all the *Prophetae* and plays about prophets. May I point out also that the *lectio* is certainly later than the *Daniel* of Hilarius?[47] At any rate the pupil of Abelard did not need to depend upon it for his material; the Scriptures and the tract contain everything necessary for his play.

As for the later Beauvais *Daniel*, it has many verbal parallels, which Sepet himself points out, with the *Daniel* of Hilarius; would it not be just as easy to assume that it is derived from the play of Hilarius, or an analogue, as to assert that it is the result of the force of "disaggregation"?

Can we follow Sepet and declare whole-heartedly with him: "It seems to me that I can easily draw this conclusion from the proofs I have given: the prophecy of *Daniel*, which one finds in the *Prophets of Christ*, has served as a base for constructing the drama of *Daniel*, which, once enclosed in the common body, finally separated itself because of its own development"? Can we believe that "there may have existed dramas of Abraham, Jacob, Joseph, Moses, David, Nebuchadnezzar, Virgil and Sibyl, formed in this way"?[48]

3. The law of juxtaposition. The selection and arrangement of the individual prophets in the different pieces which we have thus far reviewed has probably seemed to the reader the result of chance. Sepet, however, detects a tendency toward orderliness which aids him in formulating his third and last law:

We declare, however, that the chronological order satisfied

Migne, *Patrol. Lat.* Vol. XLII, col. 1124. Sepet's duty is to examine also the commentaries on the prophecies suggested by the indices of Migne.

[47] Sepet, *op. cit.*, pp. 51, 52.

[48] *Ibid.*, p. 53.

best the spirit of the pieces, and it seems that this order, which appears so neglected, has already inspired some additions other than those observed by us in the *Procession of the Ass*, additions which, in their turn, have enriched the ancient scene of the *Prophets of Christ*. In fact, the defile of the prophets is begun at Rouen by Moses, at St. Martial it is led by Israel or Jacob. Now let one begin with either Moses or Jacob, and retracing the march of time in counter-chronological order, he will find in the Old Testament diverse characters who could possibly pass for the prophets of Christ. I am convinced that in certain dioceses, Abraham, for example, had the good fortune to head the procession. The sacrifice that he was on the point of accomplishing in offering his son Isaac is, as everyone knows, a prefiguration, a presage of the sacrifice of Calvary. Abel, the first righteous person slain, Abel, gracious and touching symbol of the Redeemer, would deserve also to guide the prophets, if that rôle did not *especially* revert to his father, Adam, whose sin had rendered necessary the birth and death of the Son of God. In other words, I believe that not only Abraham, but Abel and perhaps with him Cain, Adam and perhaps with him Eve, were added to the head of the defile in good season, in certain versions which are lost to us, and that they figured there as simple prophets, in the mouths of whom the liturgist placed a prophecy, or perhaps later, a short dialogue.

The introduction of Abel into the scene of the *Prophets of Christ* is perhaps posterior to that of Adam, who would naturally introduce Abel, and who would be himself naturally introduced by Abraham. From the Father of the Hebrews to the Father of Mankind is not a great step, especially in the doctrine of the Church, where it would reflect itself in the Liturgy. If Abraham was selected by God to become the ancestor of the Chosen People, it was because the race of Adam had become unfaithful to its Creator, but Adam had been the first elect of God. They are both ancestors and precursors of Christ; the Saviour had the honour of calling himself the Son of Abraham, and was in turn called the Second Adam:

> "*Hic est Adam qui secundus per prophetam dicitur*
> *Per quem scelus primi Adam a nobis diluitur . . .*"

These two verses, which I print from the trope of the *Epoux,* explain very well the attitude of the liturgy toward the First Man; they explain and justify the presence of Adam in a liturgical drama, and make his origin integral of the office of Christmas. The first sinner takes his place properly in the midst of the prayers, songs, and representations, destined to celebrate the Birth which his sin has rendered necessary, and which God had announced to him in driving him from Paradise . . .

Once Adam and Abel were introduced into the drama and placed at the head of the procession, either they brought with them Eve and Cain, their natural companions, or these latter were added afterwards, when the rôle of Adam and that of Abel commenced to develop. It is probable that the tendency signalized by us *à propos* of the scenes of Nebuchadnezzar and of Balaam in the *Procession of the Ass*, and also *à propos* of the two dramas of *Daniel* (disaggregation), ought to have here also its effect, and exert its influence upon the new prophecies. Two little scenes, one of Adam and Eve, the other of Abel and Cain, had their being, at a given moment in certain versions which we no longer possess, in the great drama of the *Prophets of Christ*. These little scenes continued to develop, day in and day out, until they arrived at a point in their growth where they were sufficient unto themselves, and capable of being presented independently of the ancient drama, of separating themselves from the common body in order to live their own lives. At a given moment there ought to exist a drama of *Adam and Eve* and a drama of *Cain and Abel*, made *analogously* to the two dramas of *Daniel* which we have examined.[49]

Sepet's cards are now on the table and we are astonished to discover that he has been building nothing more than an *analogy* from which to argue. His ultimate purpose, revealed for the first time in the paragraphs just quoted, is to account for the Old French *Jeu d'Adam*. He hopes to show that this play in the vulgar tongue had a growth behind it similar to the sequence which he has postulated as existing between the pseudo-Augustinian *lectio* and the *Daniel* of Hilarius. Yet we have shown this *Lectio-Daniel* sequence

[49] *Ibid.,* pp. 84–86.

as insecure as a carelessly built staging: dare we build further upon it? Dare we postulate, in addition, the prophet-liturgy of Adam, and of Abel, and of Abraham, and the *long development* of that liturgy to complete the proof? For it is only when this long evolutionary process is complete, that the two dramas, *Adam and Eve* and *Cain and Abel*, are placed in juxtaposition to the *Prophets of Christ*, "thus giving us our version of the *Adam*." [50]   A final glance at the *Lectio-Daniel* analogue may put us on our guard in the last and most important issue raised by Sepet: Is the *Jeu d'Adam* the result of evolution from the liturgy? Is this earliest surviving mystery "but an office extraordinary, dramatic, exterior, in the vulgar tongue"? [51]

Reëxamination of the *Lectio-Daniel* sequence, the analogue, takes us back to the *lectio* attributed to St. Augustine. "This," says Sepet, "is the basis for all my work." [52] I believe I can show that this *lectio* is not the source or seed of a growth but the dead end of a development.

Sepet says the "characters of the manuscript appear to be of the twelfth century." [53] An examination of his manuscript (B.N. Lat. 1018) convinces me that he is altogether mistaken. Indeed, I cannot understand how he reached his conclusion. The open and round hand of the twelfth century is familiar enough to scholars. In this manuscript the characters are smaller than newsprint, closely crowding upon each other. The system of abbreviations, the crossed *p* for *per*, the special mark for *orum*, the telescoping of familiar verbs, etc., is very highly developed. Not only are the letters with the vertical strokes difficult to differentiate, but *t* and *c* are very similar because of the crowding and the

---

[50] *Ibid.*, p. 91.
[52] *Ibid.*, p. 3.
[51] *Ibid.*, p. 102.
[53] *Ibid.*, p. 3.

tendency of letter-linking. Now, in the main, these are the features of thirteenth century paleography.[54]   Indeed, I have not the slightest hesitation in assigning the Breviary of Arles the date ca. 1250.[55]

Sepet certainly would have saved himself from grave error in regard to the dating of the Arles Breviary had he examined the explicit notice in the manuscript catalogue of the Bibliothèque Nationale:

Item MXVIII

Codex membraceus, olim Colbertinus.   Ibi continetur brevarium ad usum ecclesiae Arelatus.

[54] Edward Maunde Thompson, "Paleography," *Encyclopaedia Britannica*: "As, however, the demand for written works increased, the fine round-hand of the twelfth century could not be maintained. Economy of material became necessary, and a smaller hand with more frequent contractions was the result. The larger and more distinct writing of the eleventh and twelfth centuries is now replaced by a more cramped, though still distinct, hand, in which the letters are more linked together by connecting strokes and are more laterally compressed. This style of writing is characteristic of the thirteenth century. But while the book hand of this period is a great advance upon that of a hundred years earlier, there is no tendency to a cursive style. The particular letters which show a weakness are those made by a succession of vertical strokes, as *m, n, u.* . . . . The ambiguity thus arising was partly obviated by the use of a small oblique stroke over the letter *i*, etc."

[55] My dating was confirmed by an expert paleographer employed in the Department of Manuscripts at the Bibliothèque Nationale. It is also confirmed by other noteworthy features in the manuscript. For example, note the startling use made of the rare Spanish black ink, folio 31 recto. Note the tricolored scheme of folios 6–111. Note the ornate B sketched on folio 56 recto. The MS must be later than 1170, for folio 271 verso contains a *lectio* on the martyrdom of Thomas à Becket.

Is codex saeculo decimo tertio exaratus videtur.[56]

Dating the manuscript does not necessarily date the contents, which may have been copied from elsewhere. But in the case of a *lectio* of the Arles type the dates 1200–50 are certainly early enough for the first celebration of this rite in France. We are particularly fortunate in that we can trace with more than usual accuracy the history of this lesson, for it apparently had its origin in the papal chapel. The *lectio* is first mentioned as the fourth lesson for the vigil of Christmas in the *Ordo Romanus* of Canon Benedict,[57] who was a canon of the basilica of St. Peter's and "Romanae Ecclesiae Cantor." Now it is highly likely that it was Canon Benedict himself who selected portions of the pseudo-Augustinian tract and the Sibylline verses [58] to make the *lectio* we are discussing. For while Canon Benedict assigns five lessons to the Christmas vigil in his *Ordo*, all save the fourth may be found in the earlier *ordines*. Furthermore, Benedict is specific in the matter of presentation only in regard to this fourth lesson.[59] Here alone the choir needs to be told how the *lectio* shall be performed. Consequently it may be assumed that his one innovation was this fourth lesson.

Benedict's *Ordo Romanus* was written shortly before 1143 [60] and reflects, of course, the pontifical usage of that time. Since it has never been asserted that the liturgy

---

[56] *Catalogus Codicum Manuscriptorum Bibliothecae Regia,* Paris, 1744, Pars III, t. III p. 82.

[57] Cf. Migne, *Patrol. Lat.* Vol. CLXXIX, cols. 731–62.

[58] Migne, *op. cit.,* Vol. XLII, col. 1123 ff., chs. 11–16.

[59] Migne, *op. cit.,* Vol. CLXXIX, col. 737: "Quarta lectio, sermo S. Augustini, *Vos, inquam, convenio, o Judaei.* In quarta cantantur sibyllini versus," etc.

[60] Pierre Battifol, *History of the Roman Breviary,* p. 121.

actually used in St. Peter's was a direct source of the
drama, this dating does not give us a great deal of help.
What we need to discover is, when the *lectio* was introduced into France, where it is alleged to have influenced
the drama. The ritual of Benedict's *Ordo* never enjoyed
the distinction of a papal decree enjoining its utilization
upon the diocesan churches. It was not in the strictest
sense an *Ordo* at all, but part of a larger treatise describing
the authority and dignity of the Pope.[61] As such, it did
not represent a completely revised ritual for the use of all
the churches, but rather a summary of such normal additions to the old Roman rite as had been made at St.
Peter's in Benedict's time.[62] Had it been a regular *Ordo*,
enforced by papal decree, we might have some basis for
dating its use in France. For example, the so-called "modern office" of the curia, created about 1205,[63] did not enjoy
performance in France until thirty-five years later, when
its adoption by the Franciscans assured its success.[64] But
there was no reason why any French church should exactly
duplicate the *Ordo* of Benedict. If the practice of St.
Peter's was ever imitated elsewhere, it was either because
all the diocesan churches celebrating the Gregorian ritual
enjoyed a single liturgy with individual variations, or because some one church chose to imitate a single feature of
the current Roman office which it admired. Our task is to
find the probable date for the imitation by a few French
churches of a single feature of Benedict's *Ordo*, namely, the
recitation of the pseudo-Augustinian *lectio* during the

[61] Herbert Thurston, *Catholic Encyclopedia*, "Ordines," Ordo XI.

[62] Battifol (*op. cit.*, p. 120) uses this *Ordo* to illustrate how little
change was made in the Roman rite in the twelfth century.

[63] Battifol, *op. cit.*, pp. 158, 159.

[64] *Ibid.*, p. 120.

Christmas vigils. We have just assumed that the years 1200–50 were more likely to have witnessed this innovation than any earlier period. What are the reasons for this assumption?

In the first place, this dating would allow sufficient time for the rite to become traditional in Rome, thus furnishing it with the prestige to make its way elsewhere. Since the See did not require the adoption of this *lectio,* it is reasonable to assume that it took a longer time for this piece to find a place for itself than did any single feature in the "modern office." This dating offers an interesting agreement, in the second place, with that of the *Prophetae* of the St. Martial of Limoges type. I have dated this latter piece, 1180–1200. Originating more or less in the same manner from the pseudo-Augustinian tract, it is hardly likely that they were greatly separated from each other in point of time. That the trope should appear before the *lectio* in France is in keeping with the fact that the monastic churches were quicker to accept innovations than the diocesan. Finally, this dating covers precisely all the known examples of this *lectio* in the French liturgy.[65]

Of the six known adoptions of the *lectio* in France, all in the thirteenth century, that found in the Breviary of Arles (and produced by Sepet as the earliest) may very well be the first. As I have shown (see page 70), whoever made the *lectio* in the Arles Breviary worked directly from the pseudo-Augustinian tract.[66] In this sense, he was an innovator, originating his own rite. And in this sense, he

[65] *Cat. Cod. MS Biblio. Regia.* Vol. III, ch. 3, p. 99, item MCCLV. Edmund Marténe, *De Antiquis Ecclesiae Ritibus,* Vol. III, ch. 13, p. 95.

[66] It would appear that the rubrics *Jeremie* and *Isaie* had been copied from the chapter heading *ex Isaia et Jeremia* of the tract.

may have been the first to introduce it into France. Arles, a conservative community and center of the attack against the heretics in the south (note the nature of the *lectio*), would have been likely to imitate a rite coming from St. Peter's. Proximity to Limoges might argue for some influence being exerted upon the Arlesian liturgist by the monastic *Prophetae*. But of course there is no necessary connection between the two pieces. Until some further evidence can be produced, it seems reasonable to assume that the dates 1200–50 are satisfactory for the introduction of the *lectio* in the French liturgy.[67]

Completely dated, Sepet's evolutionary process looks like this:

	Sepet's dates	*Probable dates*
Augustinian *lectio*	Eleventh century	1200–1250
Daniel (Hilarius)	*No comment*	ca. 1125
St. Martial trope	Twelfth century	1180–1200
Rouen *Processional*	Thirteenth century	1200–1250

Instead of presenting us with a sequence of material, a natural progression of illustrative documents, an evolutionary process, as he thought, Sepet has offered us scattered items which really do not form a chronological series at all. In the first place, he has arbitrarily taken as the source for his development a liturgical rite of dubious popularity, ignoring a longer treatise which not only contains the very phraseology of his document, but also was better known. He has not shown why the St. Martial trope could

[67] In passing, it should be observed that, since the *lectio* had its origin at Rome, its performance at Arles was the acme of conservatism. Nothing in this connection would argue for the type of dramatic performance which either Sepet or Chambers has suggested. Finally the scattered adoption of the lectio in France makes it dubious as the source for all the Old Testament plays.

not have been derived from this treatise as well as from the *lectio*. He believes the Rouen *Processional* to be a rite at the end of a long development. Yet, as we have seen, it may very well have been contemporaneous with the Arles *lectio*. Accepting the usual dating for this *Processional* (1200–50), he makes it the preliminary step to plays of the type of the *Daniel* of Hilarius, which must have been written a full century earlier. Indeed, the *Daniel* is so early that it would appear to antedate even the first performance of the *lectio* in St. Peter's (ca. 1143). Finally, there is considerable evidence that Sepet did not thoroughly understand the nature of the ceremonies which he was describing. Certainly, in the special sense which he gave to the word, there is no "evolution" of the drama from the liturgy. I believe that a study of the *Jeu d'Adam* will further bear this out.

Chapter VI

THE JEU D'ADAM

Its Date and Popularity; Prophets of Doom and Prophets of Christ

PROFESSOR PAUL STUDER, after a careful study of the language, places the Old French *Jeu d'Adam* "within the period 1146–1174."[1] Sepet himself would carry the play still further back, dating it in the "epoch of the *Chanson de Roland.*"[2] Apparently he saw no inconsistency in this. But even conceding that the date given the play by Professor Studer is one more nearly correct, we should be perplexed to see how the *Adam* could have evolved by slow steps from a rite which, although created in Rome about the year 1143, apparently was not celebrated in France until the thirteenth century. That is, allowing Sepet the maximum amount of time which could have elapsed between the creation of the pseudo-Augustinian *lectio* for St. Peter's and the appearance of the *Jeu d'Adam*—at *most* thirty years,—can we believe that in this brief interim the *lectio* was transported to France where it underwent all

---

[1] *Le Mystère d'Adam*, ed. by Paul Studer, Modern Language Texts, French Series, Manchester University Press, 1918, p. lvi. Studer favors the earlier date.

[2] *Les Prophètes*, p. 53. Of course Sepet would have given the *Roland* a somewhat earlier date than the best French scholars now assign it.

the processes—assimilation, amplification, disaggregation, and agglutination—which are a part of Sepet's conception of evolution? Sepet's own dating of the different pieces which he has produced as evidence shows that he considered *two hundred years* necessary for such a liturgical evolution![3] Now it would appear that the early date of the *Adam* precludes not only the idea of an evolution from the liturgy, but also makes it doubtful if any considerable influence was exerted by any liturgical rite upon the play. Such a conclusion has already been suggested by the study of liturgical history; it is reinforced by other considerations.

Sepet showed his only sign of wavering at the most critical stage of his argument. He failed to convince himself that the source of the *Adam* was wholly the pseudo-Augustinian *lectio*, or even an earlier prose version of that *lectio*. He admits a poetic ancestor, but maintains stoutly that it was liturgical.[4] Anyone who reads the play will concede that a rimed Latin poem was known to the author,[5] but he will not necessarily agree with Sepet that this poem was liturgical, that it had the same theme as the *lectio*, or that it is the source of the author's inspiration.

Certain striking features in the *Adam* appear to bear out

[3] *I.e*, from the *lectio* to the *Processional* and beyond.

[4] *Les Prophètes*, p. 87: "Dans certains diocèses, cette version en prose a persisté à cote des versions en vers; comme ces dernières, elle a reçu des additions et subi des changements, etc."

[5] Prefixed to Aaron's prophecy is the following stanza:

> Hic est virga gignens florem
> Qui salutis dat odorem;
> Hujus virge dulcis fructus
> Nostre mortis terget luctus.

Is not the theme of this poem that of the *Prophets of Doom?* Was there a long Latin poem on this subject? See text below, p. 102.

Sepet's assumption that the play is only "an office extraordinary, dramatic, in the vulgar tongue, having a part in the prepared rejoicing for piously celebrating the fête of Christmas." [6] Some satisfactory disposal has to be made of three separate points, showing apparent resemblance to the liturgy, by anyone who opposes Sepet's views: (1) the play contains a procession of the prophets, which constitutes the third act; (2) this is preceded by a rubric which, Sepet asserts,[7] links the play directly to the Arles *lectio;* (3) other rubrics call for a chorus to sing different Latin chants at various points in the drama.

Yet it is hard to reconcile the belief that the *Adam* was an office presented outside the church [8] in the vulgar tongue with Sepet's statement that "the introduction of the vernacular was gradual in rites of this kind" [9] and our own study of the degeneracy of the liturgy, of the effect of rime and acting upon that liturgy, etc. Harder still is it to appreciate the element of "pious celebration" in what appears to be a very lively drama. The chants are only six in number and make a much less vivid impression when they are read in their context in the play than they do upon the reader who sees them segregated and stressed in Sepet. Is it not possible that they have no generic connection with the drama, but are externals added by someone who wanted to give the whole a religious appearance which perhaps by itself it did not have? A comparative study of these chants with the lessons accompanying them in the breviary would quickly convince one that they are but carelessly

[6] Sepet, *op. cit.,* p. 103.   [7] *Ibid.,* p. 94.

[8] The first rubric of the *Adam* states that the play was given on the church porch. Cf. Studer, *Le Mystère d'Adam,* etc., p. 1.

[9] Sepet, *op. cit.,* p. 113.

and imperfectly adapted to the play. We have not the book from which they were selected, but judging from the Roman Breviary, they were chosen at random and from the office of the *Septuagessima*.[10] If this is a Christmas office, why are no Christmas responses selected? Moreover, these chants do not appear to be as important as Sepet has made them out to be. Songs between the acts of a modern play do not make it an opera; neither do these responses make the *Jeu d'Adam* a liturgical rite. Decidedly, upon the evidence which he has offered, we cannot concur with Sepet that the author of the *Adam* must be a cleric because he "understood so well the science of the liturgy."[11]

The rubric which precedes the third act of the *Adam* needs, however, our full attention. Here it is:

Tunc erunt parati prophete in loco secreto singuli, sicut eis convenit. Legatur in choro: *Vos, inquam convenio, o judei*, et vocat eum per nomen prophete, et, cum processerit honeste veniant, et prophecias suas aperte et distincte pronuncient.

This rubric enjoins the reading of some passage which begins with the words, *Vos, inquam, convenio, o Judei*. Is this passage the beginning of the *lectio* which opens with the same rhythmical period? That, of course, is impossible if the arguments which I have advanced for the date and origin of the *lectio* have any weight at all. Is the passage possibly some trope, similar to that of St. Martial of Limoges in theme, but differing greatly in language? But how should we be justified in assuming the existence of such a trope? Knowing the conservative tendency in such things, why should we not suppose that all the tropes on this theme would adopt the same language, or very similar

[10] Printed in Sepet, *op. cit.*, pp. 104–7. This office apparently was never troped.

[11] *Ibid.*, p. 115.

language? Furthermore, the date which I have deduced for the first appearance of all such tropes is 1180–1200, far later than the document we are discussing. Finally, may not the *Vos, inquam, convenio, o Judei* be the first line of the eleventh chapter of the popular tract attributed to St. Augustine, the *Sermo Contra Judaeos, Paganos, et Arianos?* Was there any taboo or edict forbidding the dramatist to employ this tract? Then why does Sepet ignore the possibility altogether? Let us ask ourselves, furthermore, if the use of the *Vos, inquam, convenio, o Judei* is liturgical in the play. Is it not employed possibly as a sort of Mumbo Jumbo invocation in somewhat the same way in which Faustus conjures up Mephistopheles in Marlowe's great play? [12] It must not be forgotten that the Jewish prophets thus invoked were presumably in limbo at the time and that popular belief would demand some such incantation. It is hardly conceivable that the Latin would have been understood by the audience in either case, hence the context of the passage was of less consequence than the sound. From the nature of the play, as will be seen in a moment, we can conclude that here the dramatist wanted credulity and awe, not reverence. This rubric is, then, scarcely prima facie evidence, as Sepet apparently assumes, to warrant calling the *Adam* "a liturgical office."

The third likeness (I have purposely handled these likenesses in inverse order) which Sepet noticed in the *Adam* is the procession of the prophets. The prophets present in the drama are Abraham, Moses, Aaron, David, Solomon,

---

[12] In the Chester *Harrowing of Hell*, Jesus employs Latin with possibly the same effect in view: *et dicat Jesus: "Attolite portas principes vestras, et elevamini portae aeternales, et introibit Rex Gloriae."*

Balaam, Daniel, Habakkuk, Jeremiah, Isaiah, and Nebuchadnezzar. Those absent in the *Adam* but found in the
lectio are: Israel, Elisabeth, John the Baptist, Virgil, and
Sibyl. But notice that the prophets of the *Adam* are, with
the excusable exception of Nebuchadnezzar,[13] all Jews—
exactly what the invocation demands. The author of the
lectio included Christians and Pagans in the list to suit his
purpose. If the line *Vos, inquam, convenio, o Judei*, specifically invoking the Jews, belonged to the original source
of all the prophet material (verse or prose), the *Adam*
selection of prophets is closer to that original than the
lectio selection.

Now it will appear that Sepet made an inexplicable
blunder in studying the *Adam*. He calls the prophets of
the *lectio* and tropes, prophets of Christ. *But the prophets
of the* Adam *are the prophets of doom or judgment, and
as such could have had no connection with the liturgical
office of Christmas or the joyous celebration of that season.*

This is abundantly clear from the simplest sketch of the
play. Act I represents Adam's sin, expulsion and death.
It closes with the satanic imps driving him and Eve down
hell-mouth to await the day of doom. Act II stresses the
virtue of giving one's best to the church, but it reiterates
the theme of sin and its expiation, for Abel (*sinner* through
his father Adam, and never a prefiguration or prophet of
Christ), meek in bearing, is conducted off by devils to
await that same judgement, his brother having gone off
ahead howling. Act III brings the prophets to announce

---

[13] From the fact that Nebuchadnezzar conquered the Jews (2
Chron. 36) and from the further fact that he acknowledged the
eternal domain of the God of Israel (Daniel 4), he is sometimes
referred to as a Jew. This would justify his inclusion by the dramatist among the Hebrew prophets.

the day of doom when Christ shall sit in judgement. The march of these prophets is from their "secret place," across the stage, and down hell-mouth, where they too will abide the judge. The play closes very fittingly with a long recitation of the signs which shall precede the day of doom. Considered in this light, the *Adam* is a unified treatise on sin and its punishment; regarded in any other way, the drama is incomplete and ends in the air. The *Jeu d'Adam* is not (as has often been asserted) the first three episodes of a longer mystery cycle recounting Biblical history, but a closely knit piece with an entirely different *motif*.

Singularly enough, the pseudo-Augustinian *lectio* closes with a prophecy of Sibyl, in this instance sung, which gives the fifteen signs of judgement. But the Sibyl's prophecy is also a Latin acrostic,[14] and it is the significance of this acrostic which the wiseacre of Arles stresses:

Hic de Christe navitate, passione et resurrectione, atque secundo ejus adventu ita dicta sunt ut si quis in Greco Capita horum versum discernere voluerit inveniet: *Ihesus Christus, Yos Theu, Soter,* quod, in latino ita interpretatur: *Jhesus Christus, filius Dei, Salvator . . .* etc.

That is, in the *lectio*, the significance of the fifteen signs of doom is totally ignored, while the prophecy of Christ, Son of God, and Saviour (*the acrostic*) *receives all the force* that the writer can give it. The trope of St. Martial of Limoges also stresses the coming of the Christ as Saviour, and that of the Benedictine monastery of Kloster-Neubourg

---

[14] Cf. G. Nolle, "Die Legende von den Fünfzehn Zeichen vor dem Jugsten gerichte." *Beiträge zur Geschichte der Deutschen Sprache und Literatur,* herausgegeben von Paul und Braune (Halle, Niemeyer, 1879), Vol. VI, pp. 412–76; Rudolph Peiper, "Quindecim signa ante iudicium," *Archiv für Literaturgeschichte,* Leipzig, Teubner, 1880, Vol. IX, pp. 116–37.

definitely links the prophets with the birth of Jesus. *But there is no acrostic, or reference to the acrostic, in the Adam.* On the other hand, I have never found the theme of the *Adam* in the troped liturgy of either the Monastic or the Roman church.

The author of the Arles *lectio* is wholly conventional in making the prophecy of Sibyl a prophecy of Christ and not of doom. The outstanding authorities on church doctrine, Augustine, Bede, Isidore of Seville, had so decreed. The liturgist of Limoges and the ecclesiastic of Arles appear to have been content with the conventional interpretations of these scholars. As a result, between the esoteric meaning of the acrostic and the plain sense of the text, the *lectio* presents greater incongruity than Sepet has charged to the *Adam*.

There must have been a large popular literature on the signs of doom which, like the *Adam*, made no use of the acrostic. Studies have been made of the surviving examples of this literature, and it has been classified according to the variations in the signs and the arrangement of the signs. It has been discovered that the fifteen signs in the *Adam* belong to a special group of popular origin in the early Anglo-Norman literature.[15] The *lectio* and the tropes do not follow this type; hence a poem similar to the pseudo-Augustinian *lectio* could not have been the source of the *Adam*.

The type of prophecy in the *Adam* was common property from the tenth century on. Everyone knew the signs of doom and the prophecies of doom.[16] It is not without

[15] Nolle, *op. cit.,* Vol. VI, pp. 442, 470 ff. "Typus V," p. 448 ff.

[16] "Dom Vaissette cites eight documents of this period all beginning in this fashion: 'The end of the world approaches, *and already have appeared some of the signs manifesting its imminent ruin.*

significance for our study that the persecutions of the Jews should likewise begin about the year 1000 when the fear of doom had given the signs unusual significance.[17] Thus in the popular mind these omens may have come to be connected with the hated race. It was only a step from this association to the conception of a procession of Jewish prophets forecasting the Judgement Day, the conception which is the background of the *Adam*.

No doubt the fear of doom, aroused by superstitious churchmen before 1000, was emphasized by avaricious ecclesiastics in the years 1100 and 1133.[18] Moreover, the signs of doom were kept alive in popular fancy by another bold clerical stroke: Certainly some of the signs had appeared in 1000, and again in 1100, but through the intercession of the Blessed Virgin, and through the grace and love of her Son, the eventful day had been postponed. But the faithful were exhorted to rejoice in Jesus, give oblations at the shrine of Mary, and watch for the day. A poem with this as its theme may have been recited by jongleurs

Wishing to render myself acceptable to God, I, bourgeoise, count, or baron, give to the Church of ———— a part of my goods.'" Albert Boudon-Lashernes, *Le Vieux Puy etc.*, Le Puy (Haute-loire) Bediou-Amant, 1921, p. 15.

[17] "After the year One Thousand, when Satanic Terrors haunted men's minds, it was generally admitted that the Infidels, either Saracens or Jews, were incarnations of the Devil; to avenge God, Crusaders set forth against the former, but beforehand, and on the spot, the latter were exterminated. These massacres formed an intermittent custom in the Middle Ages; when the population was afflicted with a scourge, they accused the Jews." Edmond Haraucourt, *Medieval Manners Illustrated at the Cluny Museum*, Paris, Larousse, 1912 (204 pp.), p. 137.

[18] The years 1033 and 1133 were auspicious since they fell 1000 and 1100 years after the death of Christ. Cf. Boudon-Lashernes, *op. cit.*, p. 15 ff.

in the employ of the churchmen. Certainly some such explanation must account for the Anglo-Norman *Dit du quinze signes* and for the rimed prophecy of Aaron, in Latin, which appears before his speech in the play:

> Hic est virga gigens florem
> Qui salutis dat odorem;
> Hujus virge dulcis fructus
> Nostre mortis terget luctus.

It is hardly necessary, then, to suppose that the author of the *Adam* had any liturgical precursors, since much of the subject matter of his play was in a sense public property. Indeed, is it not more logical to suppose that the true source of the *Adam* lay in this popular knowledge of the signs of doom, rather than in the misinterpretation of the theme of the *lectio*? The author of the *Adam* employed even the tract only once, and that time to introduce Act III.

Among his certain source material was the Anglo-Norman *Dit du quinze signes*. The existence of this poem, as I have stated, is not a matter of speculation. Its progeny probably ran into the hundreds in Provençal, Old French, Middle English, and High German.[19] Some of these works indicate how easy it would have been for our dramatist to discover his theme. Thus the *motif* of the *Adam* is outlined in the Middle English poem found in MS Cotton Caligula A II, which definitely connects Adam's sin with the day of judgement and Christ's redemption of mankind, although 200 lines out of 349 merely rehearse the fifteen *signes*.

This Middle English poem is further important, in that it clearly shows the theme of the *Adam* to be distinct from

---

[19] See the lists in Nolle, *op. cit.*, Peiper, *op. cit.*, Wells, *A Manual of the Writings in Middle English*, etc.

the themes of the later mystery cycles. It is often argued that the *Adam* is a fragment of a lost cycle. I contend that had the author chosen to add anything to the play it would probably have been a scene showing the Virgin pleading for the sinners and not a sequence of Old Testament episodes. Both the poem in Cotton Caligula A II, and another poem on the same theme in Cambridge University MS Ff, II, 38, show Mary interceding with Christ to pardon mankind.[20] And the oldest of Provençal poems, a mere fragment of the eleventh century, links Mary and Eve.[21] Lack of a common theme makes it dubious whether the Old Testament mysteries, the French *Vieux Testament* for example, could have "grown" out of the *Adam*.[22]

This demonstration of source material establishes, I think, two facts: (1) difference in purport separates the *Prophets of Christ* from the *Prophets of Doom;* (2) the theme of the *Jeu d'Adam* was a popular possession as early as the tenth century. No evidence exists that the theme of the *Adam* was ever in the liturgy. The explanations given by Sepet appear to have gone by the board. Where, in all the liturgy, is there anything which even approaches the *Adam* in its display of technical perfection and dramatic skill? [23]

In summary, I have tried to show that the theory that

[20] Hermann Varnhagen, "Signa ante Judicium," *Anglia* Vol. III, 1880, pp. 533–51.

[21] A. Restori, *Histoire de la Littérature Provençal* (trans. by A. Martel), Montpelier, 1894 (175 pp.), p. 28, *Prière a La Vièrge.*

[22] Sepet, *Les Prophètes,* p. 179.

[23] Professor A. H. Thorndike is of the opinion that "a theatrical and dramatic tradition developed effectively by the twelfth century. The religious plays are not only not a development from the liturgy but they are *a deflection* of the minstrel tradition from what might have been a freer dramatic development."

the mystery plays were based upon, or evolved from, the liturgy of the Church, is unsound for many reasons. The critics who were chiefly responsible for formulating the theory were prejudiced by the dubious analogy of the theater of antiquity; they were swayed by the intellectual fashions of their day; they made no serious study of the liturgy. A review of the history of the liturgy shows the dramatic incursions into the ritual to have been slow, and the actual degeneracy of the rites much later than the presence of pieces in unmistakably dramatic form. A reëxamination of certain pseudo-liturgical pieces raises the suspicion that they have been contaminated by extraneous mimetic performances, probably of minstrel origin. The documents which have been presented to establish a case for the evolution of the drama have sometimes been wrongly dated or misinterpreted. Apparently obvious source material has sometimes been ignored. Careful examination has occasionally revealed the most startling differences where close resemblances have been claimed. Finally, I have tried to show that the *Jeu d'Adam* not only is unrelated to the late liturgy of the *Prophets of Christ*, but that it is equally unrelated to the mystery cycles. In a word, the growth theory appears inadequate to account for either the *Jeu d'Adam* or the mysteries.

Chapter VII

THE MYSTERY CYCLES: GROWTH OR COMPILATION?

SINCE Sepet first stated his theory, critics and scholars have been chiefly concerned in amplifying it. Sepet himself was not a pronounced extremist: he merely applied the most striking scientific discovery of his day to the medieval drama. Yet, as I have tried to show, evolution blinded his critical faculties. It caused him to assemble his facts in a preconceived pattern; it deceived him as to the true nature of the *Adam*. But his disciples, almost without exception, have been ardent evolutionists, and they have formulated the most complicated theories of "growth" in the medieval drama, which conjectures are even more open to suspicion than Sepet's theory.

It is with these derived or modern theories that I have the greatest quarrel. Hypothetic "parent" cycles, elaborate theories based on "lost" plays, twelve thousand lines in complicated stanzas "growing" out of twenty-two Latin words—these contentions, frankly, seem to me to be absurd. And it is hard for me at times to realize the need of refuting hypotheses which on their face challenge credulity. But if I can show that a moderate and careful statement of the evolutionary theory is open to question or "not proved," have I not in a very definite way increased the doubt as to the soundness of the more advanced hypotheses?

As representative of the moderate "growth" theories which are an amplification of the Sepet case, but applied to the mystery cycles, I choose the following opening paragraphs of Professor F. W. Cady's "Liturgical Basis of the Towneley Mysteries": [1]

Two theories of greatest interest concerning the origins of the Towneley plays are those of Professor Davidson and Professor Hohlfeld. A third, advanced by Mr. Pollard, is practically the same as Professor Hohlfeld's, with one or two slight modifications, which need not concern us here.

Professor Davidson's theory is, in one respect, peculiar. He thinks the Towneley cycle to be the work of a single compiler, working in couplets and quatrains, and drawing his plays from various sources. Subsequent studies of the nature of the cycles, however, have proved them to be, not the work of single editors, but a growth, a gradual accumulation of the work of a number of editors. A closer examination of the cycle reveals the fact that Davidson's editor working in couplets and quatrains was in reality two, one using couplets, and the other quatrains, and that a considerable interval of time separated them. There is, in fact, evidence here of a certain amount of growth.

The Hohlfeld-Pollard theory, on the other hand, partially recognizes the fact of growth within the cycle. It attempts to answer two questions: What is the extent and nature of the relationship between York and Towneley?—What is the relationship between the two groups which give Towneley its importance? Hohlfeld has made a careful comparison of Towneley and York, play by play, and arrives at the following grouping of the Towneley plays in regard to their relationship with York:

(1) Word for word borrowing of entire plays: Plays 8, 18, 25, 26, 30.

(2) A general imitation of entire plays with a borrowing of isolated passages: Plays 10, 14, 15.

(3) A general imitation of entire plays without the presence of parallel passages: Plays 16, 20.

[1] *P.M.L.A.* Vol. XXIV, No. 3 (1909), pp. 419–69.

(4) A word for word borrowing of certain parts and a general imitation of others: Play 22.

(5) General imitation of isolated portions: Play 21.

(6) Parallel passages without other agreement: Play 23.

(7) Without direct evidence of any influence by York: Plays 1, 2, 3, 7, 11, 12, 13, 17, 19, 21, 27, 28, 31, 32.

(8) Not present in York: Plays 5, 6, 9, 24.

Without going into the correctness of this grouping, it is to be noted that Hohlfeld found, generally speaking, that York influenced Towneley in two ways. First, there were direct borrowings, and, second, there was a certain amount of what seemed to him general imitation, extending in certain plays to the borrowing of isolated phrases. His conclusion upon these data is that the original author (Verfasser), of Towneley was a man who was acquainted with York, from which he made direct borrowings. In certain cases he did not have a copy of these plays, but constructed from his recollection of the structure of York, incorporating such phrases as he could remember. In other cases he seems to have written independently. He always followed biblical sources closely. He was followed by another author, who wrote, with little reference to biblical sources, the humorous plays to which Towneley owes its great interest. Mr. Pollard modifies this view, giving three stages of growth instead of two, by placing in the first or earliest stage those plays in which Hohlfeld finds no direct relationship between Towneley and York. So much for theories concerning Towneley alone.

There is a third theory of the highest importance to the present discussion: the general theory of cyclical growth advanced by Mr. E. K. Chambers. In light of this theory it will be possible to discover the limitations of the other two just described. Chambers's theory is later than the two just given. It is applied to no special cycle, but attempts to outline a course of development which is common to all. Hohlfeld and Davidson, as well as other scholars, recognize that the ultimate source of the cycles was in the liturgy of the church; but they do not concern themselves with tracing the connection between the liturgical and the guild plays with any exactness. It remained for Chambers to collect the data on this larger question. A statement of his conclusions is a statement of his theory. He believes that the growth of a cycle is a literary *evolution* embracing three periods:

1. *Liturgical.* The development within the liturgy of plays on Christ's Birth, Resurrection, and possibly his Passion.

2. *Transitional.* The secularization of these plays by the translation into the vernacular and by enlargement, either within already existing scenes, or by the addition of new scenes from biblical or apocryphal history; until the cycle came to embrace the whole cosmic order from Creation to Judgement. The completion of this historic cycle closes this period.

3. *Final.* Secularization of the plays is complete. They are in the hands of the guilds, where they remain, suffering constant change; acted now by one trade, now by another; rewritten and rearranged to suit new conditions; but firmly fixed in cyclic form.

Emphasis must be placed upon the fact that this growth is an *evolution.* The limits of the periods are not sharply defined. They merge into each other. Not all the cycles reached the same full development, nor did all grow with the same rapidity.

It is evident at once that both Hohlfeld and Davidson have approached the question of Towneley's growth from a different point of view than would have been probable if they had been acquainted with Chambers's theory. Their field of vision is narrower. To their minds the growth of Towneley is a question of definite authors and compilers. . . . They did not seem to realize that the ultimate source might well have been specific liturgical plays from which the cycle developed by a gradual growth; a growth in which all questions of editors and compilers can refer only to the final stages. . . . This narrow view . . . has laid open to question the conclusions at which Hohlfeld and Davidson have arrived.

I have described this theory, which Cady has summarized from the conclusions of Chambers, as "moderate," but it is only moderate when compared with some of the more extravagant hypotheses of cyclical growth. I have purposely quoted Cady's summary of the conclusions of earlier investigators merely to show that his views, like those of all hard and fast evolutionists, are extreme when placed beside previous findings. In proportion as any view is simple and yet adequate, it should be acceptable to us. Davidson's theory of a single compiler, unless it can be proved mistaken, ought to be initially more acceptable than Hohlfeld's theory of two compilers; or Pollard's, of three compilers; or Cady's, of growth. I suggest that Cady's theory at the very outset demands a credulity transcending the limits of caution.

Fortunately, a most conclusive refutation of Cady's theory of the origin of the Towneley plays has been offered by Miss Marie C. Lyle. Miss Lyle discovers and quotes extended parallels which both the York and the Towneley plays have in common with a vernacular source, the *Northern Passion*. These parallels are found in some of the plays which Cady held to be certainly derived from the liturgy. But Miss Lyle, supported by abundant proof, is convincing:

In the preceding comparative analysis, three different groups of similarities may be distinguished between the Passion plays of the York and Towneley cycles: (1) those which are based primarily upon the *Northern Passion;* (2) those which, merely suggested by the *Northern Passion* narrative, are developed further in both cycles by the use of similar details; (3) those which are not found in the *Northern Passion*. Groups (1) and (2) include incidents which were fundamental in the making up of the Passion plays. They form the basis for the chief incidents connected with the Conspiracy, the Last Supper, the Agony and Betrayal, the Examination before Caiaphas, the bearing of the Cross, the Crucifixion, Death and Burial. The similarities in these two groups, then, are due to the use of a vernacular source, and cannot be regarded as evidence pointing to a common liturgical source. Nor does it seem probable that the similarities belonging to the third group are of liturgical origin. They seem rather to be embellishments used by the playwright for dramatic purposes; in many cases, they are merely additions which a dramatic presentation of the subject matter demanded.[2]

[2] *The Original Identity of the York and Towneley Cycles,* Research Publications of the University of Minnesota, Vol. VIII, No.

Against Davidson's theory of a single compiler for the Towneley cycle, the following arguments have been advanced by the evolutionists: (1) "The large number of stanzaic forms in the English mysteries indicates the existence of early and late plays,"[3] and consequently various authors; (2) plays in which rough, original humor abounds cannot be by the same hand which composed plays in which biblical exactness and high seriousness are the rule.[4] But I am of the opinion that these arguments are not conclusive.

Great variety of stanza form could be accounted for in a number of ways. Consider, for example, the many stanza forms employed in the *Canterbury Tales*. The same motives which prompted Chaucer to adopt different patterns for the tales may have prompted the northern playwrights to adopt different ones for their plays. Davidson found some attempt in the Towneley cycle to make the verse forms fit the character;[5] Miss Smith discovered the same to be true of the York plays.[6] Finally, variety in stanzaic structure might be explained by the supposition that the dramatists worked from a wide range of source material and did not always bother to alter the forms found in the originals. Certainly variety of stanzaic structure in the plays is no sure proof of divided authorship or growth.

The second argument against Davidson's theory of a

3. Studies in Language and Literature, No. 6. Minneapolis, June, 1919, p. 29.

[3] *Ibid.*, p. 52.

[4] A. W. Pollard, *The Towneley Plays,* Intro., p. xxvii ff., E.E.T.S., Ex. Ser., 71, 1897.

[5] Pollard, *op. cit.,* intro., p. xxii ff.

[6] L. T. Smith, *The York Plays,* p. 1.

single compiler is that the humorous plays must have been written by one man, the didactic plays by another. This argument belongs to the twentieth century—to the period of over-specialization. There is abundant evidence in literary history that the same man can be both serious and humorous. Chaucer—again—was the author of both the *Prioresses Tale* and the *Somnours Tale.* Upon consideration, the two chief objections to Davidson's theory do not seem to have much force.[7]

Dr. Samuel B. Hemingway, who attempts to divide the best work in the Towneley plays between two men, appears merely to strengthen the theory of a single author. After speaking in glowing terms of the genius who made the *Second Shepherds' Play* (although he considers the transition from the Mak interlude to the Adoration scene a violation of unity), he continues:

The *Annunciation* and *Visitation* Plays seem to belong to another small group by a collaborator of quite different, but equally undisputable genius. This group is composed of Plays 1, 4, 5, 8, 9, 10, 11, 17, 23, 28. . . . A comparison of the workmanship in this play, the *Visitation,* in translations of the Canticles, for example, with that in the other Visitation plays, should prove not only the great ability of the dramatist, but also the late date of his work, i.e., that it is as late as the *Second Shepherds' Play.* . . .

"The only bit of appreciation of this second Towneley dramatist which has hitherto appeared is the praise of one detail (T. I. 269–274) by Pollard, who very appropriately compares this stanza with Rossetti. To me the superiority of these plays

---

[7] Yet this type of argument has often been employed to prove the cycles the result of growth. Miss Frances A. Foster uses it for Towneley I (*P.M.L.A.* Vol. XLIII, No. 1, p. 133); Professor C. M. Gayley (*Plays of Our Forefathers,* p. 161 ff.) following Pollard, applies the stanzaic test to the whole cycle to determine the work of the "Wakefield Master."

on the Annunciation and the Visitation over the corresponding ones in the other cycles is quite as striking as the superiority of the Towneley *Shepherds' Plays*. The most noticeable improvement is in the versification. The weak and limping line, so common in all the other cycles, almost never appears, and there is no awkward and unnatural arrangement of the words for the sake of the metre, the thought flows naturally along, aided rather than confined by rime and rhythm. There are a good many run-on lines which add to the naturalness, and in no way detract from the music. A typical example of this excellence of versification is in 11. 89–94:

> "ffor thou has fonden all thyn oone
> The grace of God that was out gone
> ffor Adam plyght.
> This is the grace that the betydys,—
> Thou shall conceyve within thi sydys
> A chyld of myght."

This dramatist also shows a great superiority of technique over his predecessors. His excellence in form and construction is well emphasized by a comparison of his *Joseph Play* with those of the other dramatists, particularly with the York Play. The two methods of introducing the narrative of the betrothal are typical of the difference between the two dramatists. In the York Play this element is dragged in without any excuse or connection; in the Towneley Play it is one of the most natural and effective parts of the play. The *Joseph Play* also proves the dramatist's skill in characterization. Joseph is quite as real as in the Coventry Play, and is an infinitely more attractive personality. In drawing this character the dramatist seems to give a hint of his own strong gentleness, and true, deep devotion.

The only flaw in this man's work is similar to the defect we have noticed in the *Secunda Pastorum*. It is again the question of transition, this time in the *Visitation Play*, and it is again the transition from original to conventional work. The first thirty lines are a charming bit of realism—the homely, family gossip of Mary and Elisabeth—then suddenly and without warning the dramatist bursts into a very beautiful translation of the two glorious canticles, the *Benedicta tu in mulieribus* and the *Magnificat*. Even if the author had followed this general outline, which contradicts the scriptural account, where Elisabeth bursts out in prophecy as soon as she sees Mary, the dramatic effectiveness . . . need not have been lost. If, for example, in the middle of a line Elisabeth had interrupted Mary with her prophetic psalm, but to have it introduced as an ordinary bit of dialogue causes a distinctly jarring note.[8]

.Now let us ask ourselves just what Dr. Hemingway wishes us to believe. Is it not that there are *two* dramatists of extraordinary ability working in or near Wakefield at the same time? He accepts the *locus* of the plays as we do; the insistence upon simultaneous work or collaboration of these two masters is his own. I grant him the unusual merits of the plays which he calls the work of the second man. They are superior in versification and dramatic technique to plays dealing with the same material in other cycles. They were probably written at the same time the *Shepherds' Plays* were written. But I cannot see why they should have been written by a man of "quite different genius" from the man who wrote the *Shepherds' Plays*. It is a case of the same interest in realistic character, of unusual dramatic power for that day. More than that, as if it were not enough to insist upon two master craftsmen in a Yorkshire town in the early fourteenth century, Dr. Hemingway asks us to believe that both dramatists make the same mistake! This is incredible, and it seems likely that the dramatist of Plays 1, 4, 5, 8, 9, 10, 11, 17, 23, and 28 must be identical with the dramatist of the *Shepherds' Plays*.

But the chief value of Dr. Hemingway's preface, and the reason for its extended quotation here, is that he seems to be the first to recognize the high merit of the plays which have hitherto been regarded as disassociated from the

[8] *The English Nativity Plays,* p. xlii ff.

comedy group. A realization of their true worth demon-
strates the greater flaw in the Pollard theory. Mr. Pollard
has distributed these plays to three or more men. That
would necessitate the belief that Wakefield had a succession of brilliant dramatists, a theory which is even less
tenable than Dr. Hemingway's. In like manner, the other
theories of joint authorship may be dismissed.[9] We in-
evitably return to Davidson's conclusions that the Towneley cycle is the work of one man.

To revert to the known borrowings in the Towneley
Plays: Are they not perhaps even better proof of a single
compiler than of divided authorship or growth? That is,
is it not as likely that one man employed, for example, the
York borrowings in different ways, as that several men at
different times were indebted to the York Plays for suggestions and actual phraseology? This is one of the reasons
why the theory of Davidson is more convincing than the
theories of Hohlfeld and Pollard. Dr. Hemingway apparently does not take into account the York borrowings. Is
it not a little improbable that both his "masters" borrowed from York, as his grouping implies?

The exponents of the divided authorship and growth
theories will, as has already been suggested, find the whole
matter further complicated by the use which the author,
or authors, of the Towneley Plays have made of the vernacular poem, the *Northern Passion*. The indebtedness, it
should now be noticed, appears to extend to plays which
have been assigned to different "growth-stages," or to different authors, by the theorists. Miss Foster's statement
that the parallels to the *Northern Passion* in the Towneley cycle are found wholly in the couplets and quatrains

[9] See the Appendix below for a discussion of Miss Lyle's theory
of a "parent" cycle for the York and Towneley Plays.

of the Capture play [10] is a direct contradiction of an earlier statement made by her in which she reported similarities through verbal reminiscence or resemblance of outline between the *Northern Passion* and Plays 20, 22, 23, and 24.[11] Why she revised this earlier opinion I cannot conceive. Miss Marie C. Lyle proves conclusively not only that the outline of the *Northern Passion* is followed in many plays, but also, what is more important, that the influence of the poem is by no means confined to the couplets and quatrains. The play of the *Buffeting*, for example, is partially written in the nine-line stanzas of the *Secunda Pastorum* playwright and has usually been accepted as his work. Yet parallel passages are found in these nine-line stanzas. Compare:

> (1) T. Say are thou godys son of heven,
> As thou art wont for to neven?
> (*Jes.*) So thou says by thy steven;
> And right so I am
> ffor after this shall thou se
> When that I do come downe
> In brightness on he
> in clowdys from abone.
> Play 21: 249–56

> N.P. If thou be god son of hevyn.
> Ihesus answerd with milde stevyn:
> "Thou sais thi self that I am he,
> And sertanly I say to the,
> In hevyn blis men se me sall
> With my fader that weldes all."
> Harleian MS 4196: 659–66a

> (2) T. Thou art worthy to de!
> We nede no wytnes
> hys self says expres.
> Play 21, 256–60

[10] *The Northern Passion*, pp. 86–88.
[11] Frances Foster, "The Mystery Plays and the Northern Passion," *M.L.N.*, Vol. XXVI, p. 160 ff.

> N.P. He said unto the jewes all:
> "Wharto suld ye more witnes call?"
> He grantes omang us all full evyn
> And says he es god sun of hevyn
> Sen he grantes till us ilkane
> Other witnes nede us nane.
> H. 672a–76

(3) [Jesus' eyes are bound, and the soldiers, mocking, strike at him:]

> T. Sit up and prophecy
> Bot make us no ly
> Who smote the last?
> was it not I?
> He wot not, I traw.
> Play 21, 411–14

> N.P. thai said thus: "tell us, if thou wate
> Whilk of us es that the smate?
> If thou kan oght of prophecy
> Tell the suth till us in hy,
> Red whilk of us smate the now
> If thou will, we on the trow."
> H. 802a–04

Play **22**, the *Scourging*, very probably has seen the hand of the author of the *Secunda Pastorum*. It has the same characteristic vigorous scenes and the characteristic nine-line stanza, riming aaaa,[4] b,[1] cccb.[3] But in addition, it has stanzaic variations which are obviously based on the nine-line stanzas. Thus there are stanzas of nine lines with six feet to each of the aaaa lines of the *frons* instead of the customary four. Then there are stanzas of four lines, riming aaaa, with central rimes, which, despite the fact that they have eight feet to the line, suggest the *frons* of the nine-line stanza. All appear to be the work of one man. Now in each of these stanza forms Miss Lyle has found parallels with the *Northern Passion:*

> (1) Pilate and Jesus tell each other of their respective powers:

T. Thou knowes I have powere
    To excuse or to dampne here

    .   .   .   .   .

    (*Jes*) Sich powere has thou noght
    to wyrk thi will thus with me
    Bot from my fadre that is broght
    oone-fold god in persons thre.
                        Play 22, 113–17

N.P. And als it es in my powere
      to let thee pas and mak the clere.

      .   .   .   .   .

      (*Jes*) Of all thi powere rek I noght,
      ffor powere hastou none of me
      Bot that es granted unto the,
      thi might es gifen to the ful evyn
      ffra my fader that is in hevyn.
                        H. 1235–40b

(2) T. He cals hym kyng in every place/
        thus wold he ever led
        Oure people in his trace/
        and our laws downe ted.
                        Play 22, 199–200

N.P. ffor king of jewes he gers him call;
      That semes als we suld be his thrall,
      And, sir, that gase noght wele about
      To make us all his underlout.
                        H. 1117–18b

(3) T.
Ye doghters of Ierusalme/ I byd you wepe nothyng for me
Bot for youreself and youre barn teme/ behald I tell you securle
Sore paynes ar ordand for this reme/ in dayes hereafter forto be.
Your myrth to bayll it shall downe streme/ in every place in this
        cyte.

Childer, certys, thay shall blys/ women baren that never child bare,
And pappes that never gaf sowke, I wys/ thus shall thar hertys for
        Sorow be sare;
The mountayns hy and thise greatt hyllys/ they shall byd fall upon
        them thare,
ffor my bloode that sakles is/ to shed and spill thay will not spare.
                        Play 22, 338–45

N.P. Ye doghters of ierusalem
And wives out of bedlem
No more now ye murn for me,
ffor no sorrow ye on me se
Bot for Youre self wepe ye this day.
And for yowre childer murn ye may
ffor the daies er cummand fast
that all ioy shall be fra ye past.
Opon yowre faders sal ye cry
And on yowre moders and say in hy,
'ffaders, whart war we born?
Wikked werdes er us by forn;
Moders, wharto war we wroght?
better war us have bene noght.'
Unto the hillis than shall ye say
And unto mountaynes in the way:
'Hilles, falles downe on us in fere,
And mountaynes on the same manere,
Doun opon us fast ye fall
out of this care to cover us all.'
And thus than shall ye say sertayne,—
'Blisced be the bodis thet er barayne,
That in this werld never childer bare.' [12]
H. 1531–48e

In view of the fact that these parallels are found in the
work of the humorist of the Towneley cycle, as well as in
work written both in couplets and quatrains, it is surprising
that Miss Lyle did not push her discoveries to their logical
conclusion—*that this one man is responsible for these
verse forms, for the humor and the realistic scenes, and for
the use of the Northern Passion in the cycle.* Moreover,
her discovery of parallels in the various verse forms deals
another severe blow to the theories of divided authorship
and growth. In conclusion, the evidence supplied by the
use of borrowed passages and incidents in the Towneley
Plays seems rather to confirm Davidson's theory of a single

[12] These and other parallels may be found in Lyle, *op. cit.*, pp.
16–25.

compiler, than the theories of divided authorship and growth.

Elsewhere I have advanced some reasons for supposing Gilbert Pilkington to be the author of the *Secunda Pastorum* and the related plays of the Towneley cycle in the nine-line stanza.[13] His name, I believe, is the only one which has ever been suggested as that of the author of any work in the cycle. If we accept Professor Davidson's theory, shall we make this single compiler our Gilbert Pilkington? I propose to reopen the case, not that I think that it makes a great deal of difference what name we give the author, but because the discussion will bring out further evidence for Davidson's theory and, incidentally, shed considerable light on the whole liturgical hypothesis.

It has just been pointed out that considerable use was made of the vernacular poem, the *Northern Passion*, in the Towneley plays. One version of this poem is found in the Cambridge University MS Ff. 5. 48, with an attached colophon which seems to attribute the poem to Gilbert Pilkington:

> Explicit Passio Domini
> nostri ihesu christ Quod Dominus Gilbertus
> Pilkington Amen.
> Finis adest mete venit explicit ergo valete.[14]

Dr. Frances Foster doubts, however, if Pilkington wrote the *Northern Passion*, for "his name is lacking in the other eight MSS of the poem so that the ascription to him rests on the unsupported testimony of this single MS, which, according to Sir James Murray, was written in 'the middle

[13] *The Authorship of the* Secunda Pastorum, *P.M.L.A.*, Vol. XLI, No. 4, Dec. 1926. pp. 810–31.

[14] *Ibid.*, p. 826 ff.

of the fifteenth century.' " [15]   Yet, she concedes, "the use of
the title *Dominus* and the elaborate capitals in which the
name is displayed make it probable that the scribe who
copied Pilkington's name in MS Ff. 5. 48 in the colophon
of the *Northern Passion* understood him to be the author
of that poem." [16]

Now I do not wish to enter into a discussion of whether
or not Gilbert Pilkington was the original author of the
Northern Passion. It is enough for our purpose that his
name is signed to the version found in our Cambridge University Manuscript. Pilkington may be the original poet
or he may have laid claim, by virtue of recitation, to a
piece written by another man, in the identical manner in
which Jehan Malkaraume appropriated the work of Benoît
de Sainte-More in his versified Bible.[17]   What I do wish
to point out is that Gilbert Pilkington's name is signed
to one of several pieces in Cambridge University MS Ff.
5. 48 which appear to have been copied from the repertory
manuscript of some professional entertainer, some clerk
like Hilarius.

For the *Northern Passion* is not the only piece in the MS
which has definite relations to the drama.   Far more significant is the relationship which exists between the poems,
The Turnament of Totenham, and *The Tale of the Basyn*
found in the same manuscript, and the plays in the Towneley cycle written in the *Secunda Pastorum* stanza.   Not
only are these two poems written in the very unusual nine-
line bob-wheel stanza which appears to have been the

[15] *Was Gilbert Pilkington the Author of the* Secunda Pastorum?
P.M.L.A., Vol. XLIII, No. 1, Mar., 1928. p. 126.

[16] *Ibid.*, p. 126.

[17] Jean Bonnard, *Les Traductions de la Bible en vers français
au moyen âge,* Paris, Champion, 1884 (244 pp.), p. 55.

invention of the author of the *Secunda Pastorum*,[18] but one of them, *The Turnament of Totenham*, contains characters and allusions found in the play.[19] Consequently, I have felt justified in assuming the poems and plays to be the work of one man, who may have made a reputation as an entertainer by reciting the *Northern Passion*, the *Turnament of Totenham*, and the *Tale of the Basyn*, before he was employed by the guilds to write the plays for Wakefield. That this entertainer's name was Pilkington is a reasonable conjecture from the colophon of the *Northern Passion*, but a further coincidence in relation to the manuscript of the plays furnishes rather startling confirmation:

To make the story complete, perhaps the only thing necessary is to show how the manuscript of the plays, once the property of a Pilkington, became the property of the Towneley family in Lancashire. This is best done by calling attention to the fact that there exists a will made by "Sir John Pilkington, knight," on the 18th day of June, 1478, in which he asks that his body be buried "in the chantry in the kirk of Wakefield," and that his brother Charles have Bradley until his son Edward comes of age. He leaves "Pilkington hall near Wakefield" to his wife, and makes provision also for "Robert Pilkington, my bastard son."

Charles Pilkington, the brother, married a lady who, after his decease, married a Sir Thomas Knight. We have the will of this Elizabeth Knyght, proved 17 Nov. 1509. From it we learn that Charles Pilkington was the guardian of Sir John Towneley. This John Towneley founded the library at Towneley Hall in Lancashire. He is the logical man to have obtained the MS from the Pilkingtons. If our theory is sound, it clears up the long-standing mystery of the possession by the Towneleys of the Wakefield Plays; it also adds to the probability of Gilbert Pilkington's authorship of the *Secunda Pastorum*.[20]

[18] *P.M.L.A.*, Vol. XLI, No. 4, p. 817 ff.
[19] *Ibid.*, pp. 819–23.
[20] *Ibid.*, p. 830.

On the basis of this coincidence, I am going to assume, for the remainder of this discussion, that Gilbert Pilkington is the name of the compiler of the cycle and the entertainer whose repertory is partially represented in Cambridge University MS Ff. 5. 48. It will not affect materially the discussion, however, if the reader wishes to call this person by any other name.

Cambridge University MS Ff. 5. 48 has yet other connections with the drama. Following the *Northern Passion*, there appears *A Tale of the Unnatural Daughter* upon the theme of the Apollonius of Tyre story of paternal incest. Now this *Tale of the Unnatural Daughter* has the same arrangement of the story as has the fragmentary miracle play, *Dux Moraud*,[21] and may possibly have served as the source of that piece. Furthermore, *Dux Moraud* is written in a stanza riming $ababab^3 c^1 dddc^3$, which is remarkably similar to the *Secunda Pastorum* stanza $aaaa^4 b^1 cccb^3$, written in a fashion to indicate the internal rimes: $ababab^2 c^1 dddc^3$. If *Dux Moraud* comes from the same hand as the *Secunda Pastorum*, we have some evidence for the existence of a person in Yorkshire in the fourteenth century who made a living as a professional entertainer [22] and dramatist.

---

[21] Printed in J. Q. Adams, *Chief Pre-Shakespearean Dramas*, p. 207 ff.

[22] The opening stanza of *The Unnatural Daughter* furnishes evidence for oral recitation:

> Herkyns now bothe more and lasse
> I will yow tell of a hevy casse,
>   Listyns I wille yow telle,
> If ye this tale wille here
> Sum gode therein ye mow lere
>   At home if ye wille dwelle.

Now both the *Tale of the Unnatural Daughter* and *Dux Moraud* suggest to my mind, with their five scenes, five characters, unhappy beginning and happy ending,[23] the definition for comedy formulated by Johannes Anglicus. Of Johannes' definition, Creizenach writes:

The most peculiar expression of medieval error in this same sphere is found, however, in the work of Johannes Anglicus (ca. 1260), *De Arte Prosaica, Metrica, et Rhythmica.* For Johannes the distinction between comedy and tragedy exists herein: that comedy is a burlesque writing, beginning sadly and ending with joy, while tragedy, which is composed in an elevated style, begins with rejoicing and ends in affliction. For comedy he laid down the rule that it must have five acts and in it there must appear five characters: the married man and his wife, the lover and his accomplice (the cunning servant or deceiver), finally, the nurse of the erring woman or a servant of the pair. . . . Especially noteworthy in the arrangement of the characters by Johannes is the fact that the old man appears as the husband and the youth as the lover of the old man's wife. Nowhere in Plautus or Terence does the case occur wherein the deceived husband has to pay the costs of the sport. . . . How came, then, Johannes Anglicus by his singular rule? The *mimus*, who in the time of the Roman Empire reached his greatest prosperity, triumphed in the presentation of adultery scenes, and, as we shall see, the possibility is not unlikely that his performance was transplanted from Antiquity upon medieval times. Even more probable is it that Johannes depended upon medieval comic recitation. In both appear five persons in the action who took similar rôles. One of these, the *Babio*, deals with an adultery story.

In contrast to other medieval theories, it is apparent that in the views of Johannes Anglicus the dramatic character of comedy stands out in bold relief. Johannes hastened to add that not always in comedy did these five characters appear, and that, moreover, an entertaining and related, but nevertheless different, mat-

[23] For a reconstruction of the fragmentary *Dux Moraud,* see Tucker Brooke, *The Tudor Drama,* pp. 27–29.

ter was sometimes employed. As an illustration, he quoted a story, the contents of which he first gave in prose, and then in 24 hexameter verses, the last of which were arranged in dialogue, without, however, the rôles being indicated in the text. In a mine in France dwelt the Cobalt Guignehocet, who prophesied to the people. A peasant asked how many children he had, and the spirit answered, two. The amused peasant retorted that he had not two but four; whereupon the spirit replied that only two of the four were his, the other two belonged to the priest. But he would not designate the two illegitimate children and urged the peasant to extend to all a fatherly care.[24]

The work of Johannes Anglicus had a wide circulation,[25] and it is possible that it even helped to spread the very tendencies which Creizenach thinks it records. I believe that in the *Tale of the Unnatural Daughter* and in *Dux Moraud* there is a closer approximation to the rules of comedy laid down by Johannes than in his own illustration, the tale of the duped peasant. Furthermore, it seems almost certain that the author of the *Secunda Pastorum* of the Towneley Cycle either knew this treatise or had worked out very similar rules for himself. In connection with this play, nothing has been more commented on than its curious close. After four scenes of burlesque, there is introduced a fifth scene[26] in which the very clowns of the previous episodes adore the infant Jesus in the manger. A

[24] *Geschichte des Neueren Dramas,* Vol. I, pp. 9–10; 13–15.

[25] Five MSS have been cited by different critics (Cf. Hareau, Vol. II, p. 27). Besides MS Lat. 11,385 in the Bibliothèque Nationale, there are three at Munich, and one (No. 4,989) in the Imperial Library at Vienna. Probably other copies exist.

[26] The scenes are clearly marked by change of place. By lines, I have arranged them as follows: Sc. I, *On the Moors,* 11:1–295; Sc. II, *Mak's Cottage,* 11:296–345; Sc. III, *On the Moors: Shepherds discover loss,* 11:346–402; Sc. IV, *Mak's Cottage: His tossing in a blanket,* 11:403–628; Sc. V, *The Moor, with open manger where lies the Child,* 11:629–754.

little blindly, one group of shocked critics have declared this to be either satire or sacrilege. A larger group are of the opinion that the fifth scene 'is a survival of an earlier development from the liturgy, to which a playwright of considerable genius has prefixed four capital scenes of burlesque.' [27] It would appear that both groups of critics have missed the fundamental unity in the *Secunda Pastorum*. As a matter of fact, the fifth scene is nothing but the "happy close" which the formula of Johannes Anglicus demands of "comedy." It will be remembered that the play begins in the approved lachrymose fashion, the First Shepherd bewailing—

> Lord, what these weders ar cold! And I am yll happyd,
> I am nere-hande dold, so long have I nappyd.

This grim wail echoes through four scenes of the play despite the tomfoolery. But in the fifth scene, having seen God and given Him their gifts, in a word, having won their redemption, the shepherds depart rejoicing:

> *i Past.*   What grace we have fun(d)!
> *ii Past.*   Come furth; now are we won!
> *iii Past.*   To sing ar we bun(d):
>   Let take on loft!

The author not only has divided his play into five scenes and kept the antithesis between the sad beginning and the happy ending as the formula specifies, but he has never allowed more than five speaking characters on the stage at one time. For the first four scenes they are the three

[27] Professor Cady (*P.M.L.A.*, Vol. XXIV, No. 3, pp. 445–46) has a unique explanation for the structure of the *Shepherds' Plays*. Observing that the structure is the same throughout for the *Prima* and *Secunda Pastorum,* he decides that it is a framework inherited from the liturgical drama.

shepherds, Mak, and Gill his wife. Then Mak and his wife are banished, not because they were too "low" for the fifth scene, but because of a critical theory or law. The five characters of the closing episode (remember that the infant Jesus is not an actor) are Maria, Angellus, and the three shepherds. Our conception of comedy may differ from that of the Wakefield playwright, but our admiration for him must increase when we understand how he excelled in what were standards of art for him.

Once we have detected the pattern on which the dramatist made his best play, we can discern an effort on his part in his other comedies to approximate that pattern. Note the similarity in design, for example, in the following outline of the *Noah Play*, the subject matter of which Professor Gayley believes was derived from the York Play:

Scene I. The forest. Enter Noe, bewailing the evil days: He has served God "sex hundredth yeres and odd,"

> And now I wax old,
> Seke, sory and cold,
> As muk apon mold
> I widder away.

Yet he will cry for himself and his fry that they be brought to God's hall in heaven. God appears above, repenting that He ever made man, and proposing to "fordo all this medill-erd with floods"; but Noe and his wife He will spare, for they would never strive with Him, nor Him offend. He informs Noe of His purpose, and commands the building of the ark. God, however, appears to be less conversant with the character of Noe's Uxor than her husband, or more tolerant; for no sooner has the Deity disappeared than Noe expresses a doubt as to how this pattern of womankind will take the news. . . .

Scene II. Noe's House. "God spede, dere wife, how fare ye?" "The best I can; the worse now I see thee." He says that he bears ill-tidings. She opines that he were worthy to be clad in

Stafford blue (like a flunkey), for he is always adread of something:

> For I dare be thi borrow,
> From even unto morrow,
> Thou spekis ever of sorrow;
> God send thee onys thi fill.

Women may well curse all ill husbands, she adds—and such a one, by Mary, has she; but she knows how to bide her time to "qwyte hym his mede." . . . And so the quarrel goes: she promising three blows for two, biting and shrieking withal, till Noe declares for a truce, for he has other work to do. She says no man shall tarry him: as for her "to spyn will I dress me!" and *exit Gyll*.

Scene III. The Forest as before. Noe falls to work upon the ark; in the first stanza lays out the measurements and bends his bones to the tree; in the second, takes off his gown and works in his coat at the mast and wonders when his back will break; in the third makes top and sail, helm and castle, and drives the nails through the boards; in the fourth, builds window and door and three chambers "as God had said," pitches them well, thanks God that the labor is fulfilled, and hies him to fetch his wife and his meiny.

Scene IV. Noe's House. "Why, syr, what ails you?" cries she. No one is hurting you, but if you feel afraid you had better run away. "There is other yarn on my reel, my dame," replies he, and proceeds to inform her of the approaching flood. She is dazed, and dodders for fear of the tale, and with her sons prepares to "trus the gear"; but when it comes to getting into the ark she rebels. . . .

The heavens open; it thunders and lightens; down come halls and bowers, castles and towers.

Therefore, wife, have done! Come into ship fast.

Uxor. Yei, Noe, go cloute thi shoon; the better will they last.

The sons' wives take a hand, but in faith yet will she spin; all in vain do they carp. "If ye like," says one more wily than the rest, probably Japhet's *mulier*, "If ye like, ye may spin, mother, in the ship." And Noe announces the second call for embarkation, "dame, on my friendship." Whereupon, Gyll—

> Wheder I lose or wyn, in faith, thi felowship,
> Set I not at a pyn, this spyndill will I slip
> Apon this hill
> Or I styr oone fote.

She changes her mind when the water "nighs so near that she sits not dry," and hies her toward ship with a "byr." "In faith, and for your long tarrying," cries Noe, "ye shall lick on the whip." She retorts, "Big words don't hurt." He bids her cry him "Mercy!" She wishes she were a widow, she wouldn't grudge a mass-penny for *his* soul; and she sees many a wife in the audience that would hail like deliverance. Noe rejoins with sprightly advice. . . . More picturesque repartee. He cudjels her and catches a beating in turn. In fine, all passion spent, they enter the ark.

Scene V. In the Ark. The parents are upbraided by three sons. "We will do as ye bid us; we will be no more wroth, dear bairns," and Noe "hents to the helm." God takes interest in the spectacle of the heavens and the rising flood. In good counsel and obedience she continues, till the "hillys of Armonye" are touched, and the voyage brought to its traditional *happy* conclusion.[28]

Thus in structure, as well as in characterization and stanza form, the *Noah Play* is similar to the *Secunda Pastorum.* Can there be any doubt that both these plays were constructed by the same hand? Yet this play is one of those which appears to have been imitated from the York Cycle.[29] Does this fact not suggest, then, that it is quite possible that all the borrowings from York may have been made by the "master dramatist"? Is there not here further proof for Davidson's theory of a single compiler?

Further, if it be granted that *The Tale of the Unnatural*

---

[28] *Plays of Our Forefathers*, pp. 168–72. Noah's house, like Mak's house, seems to have been practicable, and the scene changes from outdoors to indoors in both plays. *I.e.*, the scheme of presentation is the same.

[29] *Ibid.*, p. 116 ff.

Daughter belonged to the repertory of the man who wrote *The Tale of the Basyn, The Turnament of Totenham, The Secunda Pastorum* and related plays, then we have some warrant on yet another score for tracing further the work of this author in the cycle. For the stanza of the *Tale of the Unnatural Daughter,*[30] aa^4 b^3 cc^4 b^3, is found in the *Creation Play,* the *Cain and Abel Play,* and the *Visitation Play,* while variants of this stanza, either aaa^4 b^3 ccc^4 b^3 or aa^4 b^2 cc^4 b^2 are scattered throughout the cycle. Finally, the *Northern Passion* is written in couplets. Thus in Cambridge University MS Ff. 5. 48 is found, if we allow for variations, a parent for every stanza form which is found in the cycle. Hence, there is no reason for supposing, on the basis of stanzaic variety alone, that more than one man had a hand in compiling the Towneley Plays.

In summary, I submit that there is, at least for the Towneley Plays, as much evidence to show that they are the work of a single compiler as there is to show that they are the result of divided authorship or of natural "growth," whether that "growth" be a matter of centuries or of decades. To begin with, the evidence of Davidson has never been controverted. In the second place, the borrowings from the York Plays and from the *Northern Passion* afford quite as good evidence for the work of a compiler as for any other theory. Finally, other unifying elements are discoverable in the cycle when it is compared with certain pieces contained in Cambridge University MS Ff. 5. 48, *viz:* the *Northern Passion,* the *Turnament of Totenham,* the *Tale of a Basyn,* and the *Tale of the Unnatural Daughter.* Incidentally, some evidence has been offered

---

[30] Cf. Hartshorne, *Ancient Metrical Tales,* p. 151 ff. I have reproduced the first stanza of the poem, which, however, is slightly imperfect, in footnote 22.

to show that the cycle was made by a man to whom play-making and entertaining were a profession. He had, at least, accepted an involved theory of dramatic art, par-ticularly of "comedy." This man may, or may not, have been the Gilbert Pilkington whose name appears in the colophon of the *Northern Passion.*

CHAPTER VIII

MINSTREL AND MYSTERY PLAY: CONCLUSION

IF THE mystery plays may be considered the work of definite authors, rather than the product of a long process of development in which many shared, then a most interesting query presses itself upon us: Were any appreciable number of these playwrights professionally trained? Is it possible to show that, while amateurism may be assumed in a great deal of the work, the better plays are probably the product of trained artists, of men who had previously made a living by their mimetic abilities in minstrelsy?

In Hilarius, the author of the *Daniel*, we have already suspected an artist with such a training. The unknown author of *Les Vierges Sages et les Vierges Folles* apparently had talents, too, which make it possible to assume for him some schooling in the arts of minstrelsy. And Gilbert Pilkington also, if he is the author of the Towneley Plays, appears to have left us a repertory which might be that of a wandering entertainer. But what about the author of the *Adam?* It is not surprising, perhaps, to find some agreement among scholars that he, at least, had somehow acquired professional skill. Professor Paul Studer writes as follows:

Of the author we know nothing, not even his name, and yet his work enables us to draw certain conclusions about him. That he was a cleric in Holy Orders, either a priest or a monk, we cannot doubt. . . . For the times in which he lived, he was a fair Latin scholar, and well read in Church literature. *But he was more than all this.* He was a poet and a dramatist. In the religious drama, a *genre* which more than any was destined soon to become the special province of literary mediocrities, he occupies a unique position by combining dramatic instinct with poetic taste. In the conception and deliniation of character, the skilful handling of dialogue, in clearness and conciseness of language, he compares favorably with the best playwrights of the twelfth and thirteenth centuries, not excepting Adam de la Halle himself. His work shows mature talent, and we may assume that it was not his *coup d' essai.* Sepet even suggests that he may have been some "professor of holy pagentry," a combination of clerk and minstrel. At all events, says Sepet, *"he rimed ravishingly in verses of eight feet and ten. I would not swear that he had not made, before his drama, some chanson de geste, some poem of adventure,—who knows? In his youth before having taken orders when he frequented the circle of this or that Abelard, perhaps he composed some lively and railing songs, some roguish and biting fabliaux."* [1]

If the better playwrights were minstrels, does it necessarily follow that they wrote no sacred drama until they had taken Holy Orders? Were all "professors of holy pagentry" connected with some monastery? It seems quite as likely that, in so far as the minstrel was concerned, if there was a connection with the monastery, it need have been only a temporary one. Professor Bédier has shown that the monasteries probably employed minstrels to compose and recite the *chansons de geste* in order that pilgrims might be attracted to visit a tomb or behold the relics of some hero.[2] Is it not as probable that the minstrels were employed, without the necessity of orders, to write the plays?

[1] Studer, *Le Mystère D'Adam,* pp. xix–xxix, lvii (the translation of Sepet is mine).

[2] Joseph Bédier, *Les Légendes épiques: recherches sur la formation des chansons de geste,* Paris, Champion, 1905–13, 4 vols.

The evidence necessary to show that the monks did employ minstrels for just this purpose is apparently contained in the mime, *Le Privilege aux Bretons.*[3] In this play, a Breton, named Yvon, who cuts broom in the forest for brushes, has been maltreated by a forester. He comes to plead that his rights have been violated, because the Bretons had obtained long ago from King Phillippe the privilege of cutting broom. The monarch, who appears to be a grandson of Phillippe, listens to the plea and, upon the confirmation of his mother that the peasant speaks the truth, confirms the decree of his grandfather.

An arresting detail in the mime is this: Another Breton, knowing of Yvon's intended journey, advises as follows:

> Voire, dist Mornesi, il saura bien parlier
> L'ef beneoit aura de Saint Germain des Priez
> Si que mes de cest siecle ne li sera toilez.
>
> 11:67–69

We cannot help wondering what this has to do with the rest of the play. That a Breton peasant, who perhaps has never been to Paris, should know about the wealthy abbey of Saint Germain-des-Prés, is decidedly out of character. But a minstrel might have put this into the mouth of a peasant for the sake of calling attention to the abbey. Moreover, may not the situation in the mime have some foundation in fact? Is it possible to find a king of France whose grandfather was named Phillippe and whose mother influenced his actions?

The French king who conspicuously meets these requirements is Saint Louis. Louis IX (1226–70) was the grandson of Phillippe Augustus (1180–1223), and in his early years was governed by the prudence of his mother, the

---

[3] Edmond Faral, *Mimes français du XIII* siècle*, Paris, Librairie Ancien, 1910 (128 pp.), p. xiii.

gentle Blanche of Castile. Phillippe, in his lifetime, had been very active in the northwest of France, had wrested Normandy from the English, and had obtained a large share of Flanders and Belgium; beyond a shadow of doubt he was well remembered in Brittany. Our minstrel and the abbey of St. Germain-des-Prés appear to be profiting from this memory and from the reputation of Saint Louis. The Boy-King, because of his kindliness and his readiness to listen to all pleaders, was hailed as the redressor of all the popular wrongs in France. The *Privilege aux Bretons* was recited throughout Brittany, I believe, in order to influence the simple but thrifty peasant of that province to make a pilgrimage, not directly to a shrine, but to his king. The Breton in the mime, aroused over a fancied injury or willing to resurrect old claims because of new promises, sets out for Paris. He is told that he must certainly stop at the abbey of Saint Germain-des-Prés, *directly on his road and just outside the walls of the city, to partake of the consecrated water, if he wants his suit to succeed!*

The hidden purpose of the mime which we have just examined was apparently, then, to direct pilgrims to a certain shrine, but it is probable that the monks employed the minstrels more frequently to keep the local communicants at home, to provide them with instruction and entertainment. This would explain why not a few of the early plays contain attacks on the *chansons de geste* which were calculated to lure the members of a constituency away from the local church. Thus in the *Adam:*

> Mult par est plain de covertié
> Que de Deu n'a nul pitié;
> Plus volentiers orreit chanter
> Come Rolant ala juster,

> E Olivier son compagnon,
> Qu'il ne ferrait le passion
> Que suffri Christ à grant haban
> Par le pecchié que fist Adam.

Undeniably related to the earliest plays through similarity of subject matter, identity of purpose, and antipathy to the *chansons de geste,* is the narrative recitation, the long biblical poem so popular in the Middle Ages.[4] In MS B. N., fonds français, 763 (folios 211 to 277) exists a paraphrase of part of the Bible in Old French verse, which, because of its appeals to listeners (*signor,* etc.), is the work of a jongleur. I quote the opening lines of the poem from the manuscript:

> Par cels quarels vont chantant
> Et d'Olivier et de Rolant
> Et des desdiuz et des amours
> Et des proesces de plusor
> Et si vuellent que on lour donje
> Loier de dire lour mansonge;
> Plusor se sunt acostumé,
> A poine en saront mais osté

[4] Of all the pseudo-homiletic material, nothing is so close to the *chansons de geste* as the saint's life—the acknowledged source of the miracle plays, a type of medieval drama which I have not treated in this study. Bédier has demonstrated the relationship between the Latin *Vita* and the *chanson de geste.* (Cf. *Les Legendes épiques,* Vol. I, p. 125, and Vol. IV, p. 419). Edmond Faral has shown that the saints' lives, in the form of recitations, were given by minstrels to attract pilgrims to various shrines. (Cf. his discussion of the *Life of St. Thomas à Becket,* in Bédier et Hazard, *Histoire de la littérature française,* Vol. I, p. 6. Its author, Guernes de Pont-Saint-Maxence, was a "priestly" minstrel.) Study of the miracle play, *Sainte Crespin et Crespinien,* led Petit de Julleville to remark: "Beaucoup de mystères eurent pour objet de recommander certaines reliques ou de mettre en honneur certains pèlerinages." (*Les Mystères,* Vol. I, p. 343.) I had arrived independently at this conclusion long before I discovered this statement.

> Mas qui vodroit lassier folié
> Et oir ouvre de clergié
> Et entendre à ma parole
> Ce que j'ai apris a escole.
> Je diroie compe d'espoire
> Que doivent havoir en memoire
> Teut cil qui la loi Jhesu Christ,
> Tienent et croient ce qu'il dist.

This amounts to a confession on the part of the minstrel that, while he abjures the *chansons de geste,* he is glad to recite sacred narrative. Whether he did this for a monetary or for a spiritual fee is no concern of ours.

Having treated the events of the Old Testament rather summarily, the poet passes on to Sibyl, who prophesies concerning the wood of the cross, after which are introduced a number of miracles accomplished by the cross. The reason for this becomes apparent at the end of the poem (folio 277). The jongleur has already sung the praises of the abbey of St. Denis, which, he avows, has the best "bible" with the best stories. Now he says:

> 1. clou (de la croix) en a à Saint Denis,
> O la corone ou tresor mis.
> Je l' i veu et baisié
> Ou tesmoinnage dou clergié
> De mainte grant enfermete
> I ont li malade sante.

Is it not manifest by these verses and by the emphasis put upon the "bible" and the cross that the whole aim of the minstrel was to entice pilgrims to the abbey of St. Denis?

But there is even better proof of the connection of these poems with the drama than that supplied by similarity of subject matter, identity of purpose, and antipathy for the *chansons de geste.* Fate, which has callously permitted the destruction of so many treasures of the Middle Ages, has preserved for us a poem which occupies a position just halfway between the religious poem and the mystery play. This is the early twelfth century Anglo-Norman *La Resurrection du Sauveur*,[5] the form of which has given the critics so much trouble, for although in dialogue form, it is interrupted more than twenty times by narrative. In the light of the theory which I have advanced for the origin of the plays, an explanation for this piece seems to be a rather simple matter. We have seen that the early mysteries were created to attract pilgrims and to keep at home the parishioners of some church which perhaps was not fortunate enough to possess the relics of the celebrated heroes of the *chansons de geste*. The reader has probably wondered how pilgrims were attracted to these performances. To depend upon a haphazard gratuitous notification would have been bad judgement where considerable expense had been involved to prepare the entertainment. Is it not much more likely that minstrels were sent to neighboring villages or were posted at the crossroads to drum up trade? How could they do it? The question is answered in the *Resurrection du Sauveur*. The minstrel apparently recited a part of the play, telling how it was presented, in order to arouse curiosity. This is precisely what is done in the poem under discussion. It is a dramatic monologue in which one person assumes several rôles in order to give a foretaste of the actual drama to be presented later. Thus, though the piece gives us nothing of "la seinte resurrection" mentioned in the second line, it is not, as some critics have assumed,[6] a fragment of a longer play, but a complete piece of medieval advertising:

[5] Printed in Monmerqué et Michel, *Théâtre français au moyen âge*, p. 10 ff.

[6] *Ibid.*, p. 10.

En ceste manère recitom
La seinte resurrection:
Primerement apareillons
Tus les lius e les mansions:
Le crucifix primerement
E puis après le monument.
Un jaiole i deit aver
Pur les prisons emprisoner.
Enfer set mis cele part,
Ès mansions de l'altre párt,
E puis ciel; e as estals,
Primes Pilate od ces vassals;
Sis u set chivaliers aura.
Cayphas en l'altre serra;
Od lui seit la juerie,
Puis Joseph d'Arimachie.
El quart liu seit danz Nichodemus.
Chescons i ad od sei les soeus.
El quint les disciples Crist.
Les treis Maries, saient el sist.
Si seit purvéu que l'om face
Galilee en mi la place;
Jemaus uncore i seit fait,
U jhésu crist fut al hostel trait;
E cum la gent est tute asise
E la pès de tutez parz mise
Dan Joseph cil de Archime
Venge a Pilate, si lui die:

(*Joseph*):
Deus, qui des mains le rei Phraon
Salva Moysen e Aaron,
I sault Pilate le mein seignur,
E dignetez lui doinst e honur!

(*Pilatus*):
Hercules, qui occist le dragon
E destruist le viel Gerion,
Doinst à celui ben honur
Qui saluz me dit par amur!

(*Joseph*):
Sire Pilate, beneit seies-tu!
Sait te Deus par sa grant vertu!
                    Etc., etc.

It is easy enough to see how such a piece as the *Resurrection du Sauveur* may have been suggested by the recitations of the minstrels. But, on the other hand, it would be unwise to assume that the earlier plays were based on narrative poems. Indeed, I believe, and I have taken pains to show this in connection with the *Adam,* that the subject matter of the mysteries was so generally familiar that search for a direct source is little short of folly. I have tried to link the plays to the poems for an altogether different purpose: I have merely endeavored to show that a large body of dramatic and semi-dramatic material originated as early as the *chansons de geste* with the purpose of combating their influence. Now it may be that in some cases plays were actually built upon the narrative recitations of the minstrels. But generally the situation was probably this: where a large number of actors could be gathered, plays were given and minstrels sent out to summon an audience; where few actors could be commanded, or the church could not afford the expense of dramatic presentation, minstrels were detailed to try the effect of narrative verse, verse which contained compelling allusions to the benefits derivable from a pilgrimage to a sacred shrine.[7] Poem and play were contemporary, in so

[7] In this connection, the relationship which apparently exists between the *Stanzaic Life of Christ* and the Chester plays, first pointed out by Dr. Frances Foster, is worth noting. (*A Stanzaic Life of Christ* E. E. T. S. Orig. Ser. 166; 1926 for 1924, p. xxviii ff.) After demonstrating that eleven of the plays were influenced by the *Life,* Dr. Foster remarks that "the knowledge of the poem that the playwright shows is what would come, not from setting the English text before him as he worked, but from an intimate acquaintance with half memorized phrases." Is it not possible that both the author of the plays and the author of the *Life* were members of the famous Chester minstrel guild? Who would be more

far as we can judge from the evidence; the poverty or the cupidity of some monastic organization is explanation enough for the origin of both types of literature.

In conclusion, then, there appears to be evidence to support the view that the early plays were the work of the professional entertainers of the day, the minstrels, who were hired by the monks to entertain, to instruct, and to draw to the shrines the populace. Beyond the period of origins, it is extraordinarily difficult to say how far this practice extended, and no attempt has been made in this study to do so. Furthermore, no contention has been raised that in later times the playwrights did not occasionally go to the liturgy, as they may have gone to any other easily available source, to borrow a word, a phrase, or a theme. *But that there is any generic connection between the drama and the liturgy has been most strenuously denied. The mystery plays apparently did not originate in the Easter ritual; the seed of the drama was not the St. Gall* Quem quaeritis *trope.*

apt to memorize the *Life* than a minstrel? That the author of the *Life* was no cleric is probably intimated in the following lines:

> "By-fore every mater, and I may,
> The Auctor shal by my bone
> That clerkus shal not after say
> These newe fables wrote a fonne."

APPENDIX

"PARENT CYCLE" THEORIES

A SMALL group of critics who have examined the existing
documents, and who have apparently found no evidence to
support the liturgical theory and yet are unwilling to re-
linquish it, have compromised by suggesting the existence
of a "parent cycle" now lost. They maintain that such a
cycle contains the evidence for liturgical origins which is
lacking in the surviving plays.

For the York and Towneley Cycles, Miss Marie C. Lyle
has advanced such a theory.[1] Miss Lyle's theory is based,
I believe I can show, upon faulty reasoning. She nowhere
states her precise method of deduction, but it is easily detected. The five plays that York and Towneley have in
common belong, of course, to this parent cycle. Having
decided this, Miss Lyle then seeks to discover *the less
elaborate play in each cycle dealing with a common theme.*
Once she has determined this play, she assigns it to the
parent cycle. The following passages culled from Miss
Lyle's work prove this to be her method:

(1) *Joseph's Trouble about Mary*
These instances indicate an elaboration by York of the simple
Towneley play, and therefore, the Towneley play is not to be
regarded as an "adaptation of an earlier York play," Professor
Gayley suggests, but as the earlier play itself. . . .[2]

[1] *The Original Identity of the York and Towneley Cycles.*
[2] *Ibid.,* p. 56.

(2) *Magi, etc.*

In York, the incidents of the *Magi* or the Coming of the Three Kings and their Oblation are divided into two separate plays, whereas they are included in a single play in Towneley. . . . The difference may be explained by assuming that the Towneley play . . . represents the earlier version and the two York plays later revisions.[3]

(3) *The Flight into Egypt*

Certain York passages appear to be verbal expansions of simpler Towneley passages. . . . Accordingly the Towneley play is not to be regarded as an imitation or adaption of an earlier York play, but as the earlier play itself.[4]

(4) *Massacre of the Innocents*

In plot development, there is but one fundamental difference, that of Herod's attitude when he learns the result of the slaughter. In York he is angry because of Jesus' escape, but in Towneley, believing that the child has been slain, he rejoices and rewards the soldiers. Except for this difference, the Wakefield author merely elaborates or makes slight additions to the incidents presented in the York play.[5]

(5) *The Incredulity of Thomas*

The York play . . . probably represents the parent play, of which the extant Towneley play is a later revision. Thus the differences between the two plays may be explained. The Towneley play not only includes all the incidents contained in York but adds to them.[6]

This argument, based on the assumption that elaboration always means a later play, is on the face of it fallacious. How would this argument apply, for example, to the plays of Shakespeare? *Macbeth*, a short play, might be regarded as earlier than *Love's Labour's Lost; Hamlet*, the longest play, might by this logic be dated after the *Tempest*. For countless reasons a playwright may have desired to compress an existing play. Hence a compressed play

[3] *Ibid.*, pp. 56, 58.   [4] *Ibid.*, pp. 61, 62.
[5] *Ibid.*, p. 63.   [6] *Ibid.*, p. 67.

might appear the more primitive. This, I believe, has led Miss Lyle astray. Offhand, several good reasons occur to me for compression which I will note here as they have not been noted by Miss Lyle: (1) The playwright may have compressed borrowed material in order to have a greater opportunity to display his own work; (2) he may have differed in opinion with the other dramatist as to the relative value of an incident; (3) for purely physical reasons compression may have been necessary, *i.e.*, less time may have been allotted in one place than in another for presentation; or the number of actors available for a certain play may have been fewer in one town than in the other. If any one of these causes resulted in compression, Miss Lyle's theory would not hold. As there seems some likelihood that they all may have operated, her theory certainly is not very tenable.

BIBLIOGRAPHY

For the convenience of the reader of this volume, I have gathered in this place the more important entries in my footnotes. Inasmuch as there exist a number of excellent bibliographies, both of the liturgy and the drama, for example, in Peter Wagner's *Handbook of Plainsong*, and in Sir Edmund K. Chambers's *The Medieval Stage*, I have felt no necessity for printing an extended bibliography of either subject.

Adam, Le mystère d'. Ed. by Paul Studer (Modern Language Texts, French Series), Manchester, University Press, 1918, 175 pp.

Adams, J. Q. Chief Pre-Shakespearean dramas, Boston, Houghton Mifflin, 1924, 712 pp.

Battifol, Pierre. History of the Roman Breviary (Translated by A. M. Y. Balay, from 3d French edition), London, Longmans, 1912, 333 pp.

Bonnard, Jean. Les traductions de la Bible en vers français au moyen âge. Paris, Champion, 1884, 244 pp.

Brooke, C. F. Tucker. The Tudor Drama. Boston, Houghton Mifflin, 1911, 461 pp.

Cady, F. W. The Liturgical Basis for the Towneley Mysteries. (Publications of the Modern Association. 24: 419–69, Sept. 1909.)

Chambers, Edmund K. The Medieval Stage, Oxford, Clarendon Press, 1903, 2 vols.

Coffman, G. R. A New Theory Concerning the Origin of the Miracle Play. Menasha, Wisconsin, 1914, 280 pp.

Coussemaker, C. E. H. Drames liturgiques du moyen âge, Rennes, H. Vatar, 1860, 322 pp.

Creizenach, Wilhelm. Geschichte des Neueren Dramas. Halle, Niemeyer, 1893, 5 vols.

DuMéril, Edéléstand. Origines latines du théâtre moderne, Paris, Welter, 1897, 420 pp.

Duschene, Louis. Christian Worship: A Study of the Latin Liturgy up to the Time of Charlemagne. (Translated by M. L. McClure) London, Society for Promoting Christian Knowledge, 1919, 593 pp.

Early English Text Society:

The Chester Plays, ed. by Deimling and Matthews. Extra Series, 62, 115; 1892, 1916, 2 vols.

The Northern Passion, ed. by Frances Foster. Original Series, 147, 148; 1916, 2 vols.

The Towneley Plays, ed. by A. W. Pollard and George England, Extra Series, 71, 81; 1897.

Foster, Frances. Was Gilbert Pilkington the Author of the *Secunda Pastorum?* (Publications of the Modern Language Association, 43: pp. 124–36, March, 1928.)

Frere, W. H. The Winchester Troper. London, Henry Bradshaw Society, 1894, 248 pp.

Gautier, Léon. [Histoire de la poésie liturgique au moyen âge:] *les tropes.* Paris, Picard, 1886, 138 pp.

Gayley, C. M. Plays of Our Forefathers. New York, Duffield, 1907, 349 pp.

Ker, W. P. The Dark Ages. New York, Scribners, 1904, 361 pp.

Kretzmann, Paul E. The Liturgical Element in the Earliest Forms of the Medieval Drama. (University of Minnesota Studies in Language and Literature, No. 4) Minneapolis, 1916, 170 pp.

Lange, Carl. Lateinische Osterfeiern, Untersuchungen

über den Ursprung und die Entwicklung der liturgisch-dramatischen Auferstehungsfeier. Munich, Stahl, 1887, 171 pp.

Lyle, M. C. The Original Identity of the York and Towneley Cycles (Research Publications of the University of Minnesota, Vol. VIII, No. 3; Studies in Language and Literature, No. 6) Minneapolis, 1919, 223 pp.

Magnin, Charles. Histoire des origines du théâtre moderne, Paris, Prolégomènes, 1838, 2 vols.

Marténe, Edmundi. De Antiquis Ecclesiae Ritibus. Antwerp, 1737, 4 vols.

Maskell, William. The Ancient Liturgy of the Church of England, Oxford, Clarendon Press, 1882, 2 vols.

Mees, Arthur. Choirs and Choral Music, London, Murray, 1901, 251 pp.

Monmerqué [L. J. N.] et [Francisque] Michel. Théâtre français au moyen âge. Paris, Didot, 1839, 670 pp.

Nolle, G. Die Legende von den Fünfzehn Zeichen vor dem Jugsten gerichte. (Beiträge zur Geschichte der Deutschen Sprache und Literatur, herausgegeben von Paul und Braune. Vol. 6, pp. 412–76, Halle, Niemeyer, 1879.)

Palmer, William. Origines Liturgicae. 4th edition. London, Francis, 1845, 2 vols.

Peiper, Rudolph. Quindecim Signa Ante Iudicium. (Archiv für Literaturgeschichte. Vol. 9, pp. 116–37. Leipzig, Teubner, 1880.)

Petit de Julleville, Louis. Les mystères: histoire du théâtre en France au moyen âge. Paris, Hachette, 1880, 2 vols.

Pollard, A. W. English Miracle Plays. Oxford, Clarendon Press, 1890, 301 pp.

Sarum Missal in English, The. (Translated by Frederick

E. Warren) London, Library of Liturgiology and Ecclesiology for English Readers (ed. by Vernon Straley), 1911, 2 vols.

Sepet, Marius. Les Prophètes du Christ, étude sur les origines du théâtre au moyen âge. [First ed., 1867.] Paris, Didier, 1878, 139 pp.

Varnhagen, Hermann. Signa Ante Judicium. (Anglia, Vol. 3: pp. 533–55. 1880.)

Wagner, Peter. Introduction to the Gregorian Melodies: A Handbook of Plainsong. London, Plainsong and Medieval Music Society, 1904, 280 pp.

Ward, A. W. "Drama," in Encyclopaedia Britannica, 11th edition, Vol. VIII, pp. 475–546. Cambridge, University Press, 1910.

INDEX